FIAT LUX

Ivan Argüelles

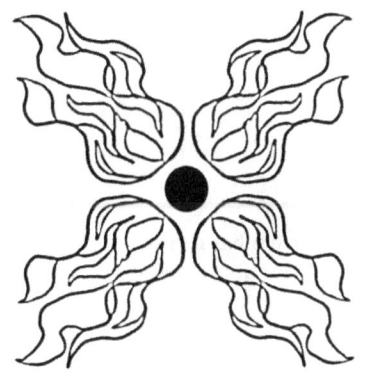

LUNA BISONTE PRODS
2014

One section has appeared elsewhere:
Juggernaut appeared in Caveat lector.

Cover art/ illustration by C. Mehrl Bennett

ISBN 978-1-938521-15-7

LUNA BISONTE PRODS
137 Leland Ave.
Columbus, OH 43214-7505 USA

www.lulu.com/lunabisonteprods
www.johnmbennett.net

FIAT LUX

Amors vai com la belluja
que coa'l fuec en la suja,
art lo fust e la festuja,
--Escoutatz!—
e non sap vas qual part fuja
cel qui del fuec es gastatz.
Marcabru

I

INTROIBO

the end which is also the beginning
the insectary of the mind
yclept γνωμων
carried over the shoulder backwards
into the river of time
ransacking the jewels of heaven
no longer interested in the mere range of languages
and their articulation
sonant clusters like gold and silk interwoven
"by the grace of Ahuramazda all that we did"
to be both deliberately filthy and obscure
and didn't we chase the merry over
loam and tide
the greater ticky bird and the lesser ticky bird
who announce the dawn of Memory
if there were a tripartite way of being
from the Giant's Causeway to Stonehenge
arousing Finn's hand again the timber trade
plowing with long ships the wide dark mere
ivory tusks cinnabar amber
and by sunset when the water turns to flecks
of copper and the tramontane blows our fleet
past the pillars of Hercules
who then will the wiser be strewn
'twixt the main and the immense invisible
did darling darker death her twill spell this yarn

and suchness of againwit beside some crystal rill
and sing sweet dust mingled sleeves the origins
fourfold flung midst sleep the heavy
one waking never knows meandering
to some dusky spore on the asia side the ancient
far from the transom's small light the gimlet bore
shaking headwinds round and round the gore
alphabits chastened scripts scribbled lore
on high beyond any orientation the stars!
little frames of gilt the sky
a god whilom peers blinded momentarily by Bang!
and in an instant or less than the myriads
of galaxies cottages garden plots rivulets fortresses
cobbled lanes ruined glass barren stretches of fire
the whole heraclitean thing asunder shivered and shattered
against the loom of language what? starts a shaggy
maundered with thought to being a whistle
as the car sheers fog lights with a tremendous metal
shining and shining can arise from ruin nothing
venereal outpost ***carnicería paraíso***
husbanded headband rainbow terrific clap by Jove
how many windows later must we brook this storm
eventide the summer mourn of can't remember when
when islands drifting melancholy once a shepherd dwelt
that was when like a big orange moon her face
it first appeared singing between slats of empire
and the eight thousand spears below and the lowing
of stellar cattle rowing across the hoof-shaped bay
and maddened at the city gate the elephant reared
to get out of that dream to run to the library
to make it Saturday again the peaceful and red brick
layered myth brazen faced with notched swords ablaze
from the rich recently plowed earth Gaia furrowed
her titanic sons wrenched muscle and hip one against
foremost the other Hooting loud the mace and fly
can such between just pages of a book?
what are the mighty against this fraction?
the tethered syllables of old Babirush in clay wedges

fix the heavens with a fierce cobalt incantation
haunted shibboleth empyrean of phonetic symbols
in arterial decay by the roadside clattered chariots
horses broken at the haunch neighing horribly
by meadows of consonant clusters fiery diapason
how can the many times we read the opening lines
the inches of constant fret and delay translating
didn't you ever think of using the telephone
would Ajax be on the other end sweating the nightmare
in hexameters of despond and reeling mist walls
cannot say what mother would be precious pearls
sounding against darkened musk room's end
argent plash the eyelid's sill a hovering remote
stilled the ever but small liquid trophy glimpsed
and diameters of hours rounding the satellite's veer
could this be the one and every historical event
smoked in the ear draining pulse of august mill
heat and its terrific reflections mirrored blackly
in the brain's volatile shuttle cock   a thing!
poems set to a music hermeneutics each note the
caught in mid flight the arrow's ornate sense of destiny
whizzing into the sump of interpretation
like the skillfully fingered flute child Krishna plays
loitering by the banks of the sultry Yamuna
so one thing leads to the other *dans la grande nuit des mots*
and soon we are kissing the front end of the next century
rapid viviparous entities that we are fast dying

Whoosh!   the assault on alphaville
bunch a goddesses come running out mostly naked
one shouts "omicron" another pleads "omega"
it's always like that an indecision in cloth
somber megaphone deliberations in one ear
siren swoon in t'other a hank of moist hair a
alone in the car radio feeling *frozen*
decades pass and the insect of obsession is still there
eating away at the detritus of
                    one with the red hair of isolation

cries out her "sigma" rolling abject whorls of
dust pans recycled for epic   junction
matter of seconds and the entire cosmos refigures itself
in ultra red time capsules distributed at a local pharmacy
we are there jostling for attention the movie camera
an agent of rushing night streams singing swinging
both fists in the plush area below the left eye
the wee hours a piano a   avenues flood
emptiness the crooner in dishabille mocks Enkidu
ever the god pawn at the mercy of the temple whore
how many deities put to death last week?
is it to till we hoe with ink the sad spell grieving
anvil sparks flashing a radiance of words forgotten
china shore sinking for miles of longing the intense
did we unhitch the horse and then to the cabildo
to sport junketing moon shrines to deaf stone
while still a fourth one in ochre beige decries "beta"
moving a picture in sepia oval tint the actress
I want her in pink each finger spawning a sigh
in the key of Delta moistened   un hunh
yes can such be crammed into a minimalist suite
mimicking the faux grammars of rhododendron and lilas
can flowers think can inscriptions mate a dueling sun
isn't it a poem to re write and learn to do it right
margins to the left and put the dactyl next to the spondee
scanning latin derivatives while Dido burns   alas
them goddesses all a mess want'um honeykins dead
**   ruin upon ruin in the square mile of marsh**
allotted to moonlight on the run to Uranus
has feet will travel reciting as well as can be recalled
the opening stanzas of the rg veda big mouth O
haven't we "seen" enough haven't we quelled
watching the red skins whomp it up on Manhatta
it is a poem re written rebus and hump backed
soliloquy in american diptych stitching muddy water
a dream I am we are all having in simulcast opticon
links letters to knuckle bone and transposes
head to gravity to make sun shine while it hays

have learned to scribble at best a few by heart
nosegays and magnificent temple wreathes out to dry
knock once for fun twice for the undertaker to fly
I am getting nervous about the hour
"they're not home yet"   sound of car wheels
on gravel crunching at the dead of night
spine for lunch asbestos orientation crushed odor of
in the beginning of the end ghosts
exactly who the brother is and who the others
rapping on sheet glass for another drink
lamba mu and nu in quick succession naked
in front of a big Japanese lens
this isn't about "you" any more this isn't
hunkered down next to the large empty pond
a Buddha type in overalls just waiting for a hit
and the goddesses half tippled with tattooed eyes
they come rushing to him making the air cry
with their lamentations over gamma and delta
"ladies why are your eyes tattooed?"
"by the brookside nude we swam in the millpond
undressed we died"   heavy with nostalgia
skin dripping a bitter map of mountains dark
why does their summer never come why does
and is it because we don't have the money nor does
whenever we approach them banshees or maenads
they flee like wildfire their various hair ablaze
smoke signals from the Hindu Kush languid dappled
on the way to Mohenjo Daro to find the dancing girl
with her tresses tufted in a white ribboned top knot
drink to her, comrades!   evening is drawing nigh
the deserted fane the stray dogs whining a lost moon
how many mansions later is it according to the Mayans?
how plaintive the oncoming night sky its Pleiades
drawing the water winch across Orion's Belt
from afar the flower song wafting light years a-coming
it is because we are learning the poem and sleep
dream-stippled bed speech shifting yellow sheets
move over,

it was here the museum was lifted
by levers into the celestial lake and paper fans
inserted into our hands asked to walk the length
of a marble parapet jutting out over the Mojave desert
and far below the threads of motorized roadways alight
toys of the puzzled mind   the Minotaur
casts his crazy shadow over the mirror
athirst for Athenian blood he stamps his cloven feet
from here to Egypt it's a swallow's flight
strange engravings in the ether bring to mind the
yes the goddesses the way they murmured in the well
brief as a slain gazelle their aspirin white breath
could try to talk tapers flickering in the back of the eye
from either side the onslaught of whispered words
of love and its trials and the castle on the mount
blade of maize, do you hear me?

switch to present, tense
   cigarette in mouth, ache in heart
me-me-memorize all of it from aleph up to zed
birds eye view of the Canadian Rockies
doing a swing shift on Pluto where histing her skirts
Persephone does a fan dance the craze of the cemetery
dallied too long in the month of Furnace
singed her skirts and the knees lit up like carbons
fall in love with that pouting mouth hair all over damp
wanna go to hell,   she's the traffic girl
on channel 5 not a day older than the day she got it
carmine blur and sound of centaurs rushing sand
how to understand how to explain how to dwell
in the cusp of the Nile day-dreaming sphinx stunned
the organ grinder who works the mind's shafts
is high again   Sicilian,
                    by the rustling reeds Theokritos
laments his Bion all of a strange afternoon
eyes the color of furze and tobacco
sky pivots in them a full turn then disappears
these are the soledades great noons of grass and heat

far from the sea's reiterated echo of salty manors
when only the cicada's monotonous obsession
toils the violin of haunting and despair for hours
until from a chinese balcony the widow throws her shadow
into the waving illusion of harvested fields
no one recalls anything,   immense black shawl
floating like a transparent bat three in the afternoon
so it is, friends, the story of my love
and bows and employs the furiously painted puppets
to narrate the insanity of Orlando on the moon
is he the one who was crying by the gate last night
rust and grime pith of the gypsy street walkers
hawking their hidden jewels wounded sparrows
the phthisic breast,
to discuss the interminable the infinite the endless
and Joe at the head of the table with his condescending
all smirks and quietly aggressive completely sure of
turning to each of us dust and shadow a question
is literature the prize or immortality
enumerating the platonic virtues the origins
how the Mayo clinic came to be and the mansion on the Hill
and the many byways between school and playlot
the kids tossing a ball into the galaxies and shouting
the alley coming home backs of houses screen doors
shutting on the immense dark within
what is the distance between what cannot be and
what is here and now what is the green the reverie the
around her temple swart ivy twines
and Lo! for if I am with you today
do not think I will be forever among the flower pickers
those destined to kneel in hot fields choosing
the multicolored variety sun constructed anthology
these blooms culled are the many hued voices
that make up a lifetime of memory a longing
and browsing in the remains of Old Latin
we find that Ennius remembers being a peacock
Etruscan god of gardens Vertumnus, lead us on!
what goes dancing primrose wild and lotus calm

making the way to the forge of possibilities
to the new day after life to the tremendous
the ineffable and Joe at the head of the table
defiant somehow but nervous biting his lip
to be photographed in his post-existence glory
like when we was kids hiding behind the apple tree
a shame it all has to end and the pruning shears
rusted in the garage and the big white whet-stone
and the bottles of whiskey hidden behind
the fishing tackle
Vertumnus, lead us on!

II

EL TRONO DE LOS DIOSES

through narrow waterways deep and clear
our small skiff we ply, Jesus, yes we say sweating
still the next afternoon and no further than the still point
the engrossed unfathomable from which we cannot move,
nor does a hand descend from the menacing summer cloud
nor from nowhere the rushing voice of a deity declare,
much the same it was in the last century as shadows
playing on a stage where meadowlark and thunder sang
we gathered up our forces and for love drank deep the draught,
chill struck the brow, evanescence set in, and night,
the looming, brooded, a single verb we employ to shove
the wounded craft across the still mere into the thick tuft
of grasses greener than bottle glass and imagine, yes, this
not that is where to be is the greater dilemma, under the sky,
rent the bosom of mists and booming hollow the unknown tract
through which we must pass, yellow looming ever nearer
saffron underthoughts pale advances on air, breath!
do we shiver its extent, or excited start talking as if inspired
calling on the goddess to come forth to show her bare thigh to
if even, set the tooth on edge and smell of meat over done sifting

**through the rare ether of imagination until caught in a mud
with no traces of color we are turned inward to implore, what,
a single blade of russet grass we cling to sharing in the event
of dying the small streak it sets against the moving heavens,
small shifts in the spectrum, come to the third hour and the sun
still high, has it budged at all, silence all around except for the buzz
of an insect trapped in a web, not where we should be, not,
the ancient stone the untapped source the personification
of a lost emotion, azure hums with the flight of dead angels
whose airplanes have gone lost beyond the radar, we knew
them, we know them no more a sort of panic at the throat
and in the ear a drill perfects a childhood memory of red,
this is not the way to be, this is not the boat we hired, this
is not not, this, the wine have we drunk it all, the white and
the rosé kept chilled in the small ice bucket, no one recalls where
nor when it was last night and in a dance hall to be sure
we contacted for the first time the houri of love, dark
semblance of a desert bloom storming behind the hair
a gleaming the lightning of sand, is it any further now weight
mired in this small catastrophe of ochre mud, expect depth
and the formless activity of desire when least anticipated
to arrive waving a brief flag of suspense extreme for its
broad weave, there, I have never been farther from the personal
pronoun than now, and other things that are strange and
unpleasant to admit, losing sight of destiny the goal the long
haul toward sunset where we should be mooring at a wharf
called something like fandango or flamenco, not sure which,
and ticking within the intimacy of spanish gold a temporary
voice summons its animal, startled we wake from our siesta
drenched in the myopic heat of this false tropic bole, Amaryllis
the fair whom we share in a single uninterrupted dream
she steps out of the tangle of grasses her ankles filthy with mud
her skirts loose and ready to fall and her hair the undone
continent of Mu,**

**this waste place this sump they call *El Trono de los Dioses*
girls used to come here to draw water
pack animals on the long trek to heaven**

arms white as rope fallen asleep beside the stone work
cannot name a more like paradise in fewer words
scant allusion to a mythography of distances
eros was here kindled once bussed on the nape of the neck
and shot like a stray dog at sunset
other languages contend for the honor of poetry
metaphor and its humus of discontent
but the one spoken as rapidly as gunshot by the girls
who used to come to draw water here
to hear them speak lilting sing song broken tagalong
it seemed to the unaccustomed ear Paradise
this place called by some *El Trono de los Dioses*
bric a brac amorphous rocks set one against the other
red dust flakes off them easily and a shadow
scary for its constantly moving shape
if we could agree on the cut of the cloth
to cover her lap and send her back to the cabildo
or the plane ready to go to Miami
but here all afternoon the whining of cicadas
and the remote drone of diesel engines on hot asphalt
supposed to be a ruined temple or something
things come apart lose texture and color as dust
make a circle in the pulverized part
chant and dance up and down Hooping Hooping
soon out of pure air shaking her inky tresses
the daughter of a god will manifest
and sit herself down on *El Trono de los Dioses*
waiting to milk the evening kine

the easy part is getting the bark to move again to enter
the bottle green waterway between the immense shadows
of the palm trunks, to read the inscription on the surface
constantly wavering among water fronds and lotus when
the sun cuts its angle abruptly and the characters dissolve,
what can you do, engine of destruction, doubtlessly lost
in the moving earth, the parts that cannot be identified
that cannot have a name a history, born from the lotus Brahma
the four faced like a clock fused to all directions, of destruction,

**sun glinting on surface swarming with midges and gnats,
infinitesimal deities of malaria, characters dissolve, swift
air currents carrying messages from the dead, short circuit
of existence the lilting afterlife of a thought, first it's yellow
then verging on blue green the abyss where myth vanishes,
pushed out toward the center then start going in circles
the whirlpool, mysterious eddies almost see a face below
the surface, sun begins to decline against the hour when
we do the reading, technically dead the, of destruction,
barely perceptible the whirring of infinitesimal deities
of malaria, dissolve, reading in unison selections from
the Bhagavata Purana but in this searing light the angle
of the sun, characters dissolving, face beneath the surface,
beckoning between the immense shadows of, moving earth,
this, reflections in golden liquid shimmering of the sun his
ruddy head slowly going down, realize there is no sure exit
the snaking waterways between gilded crests of shadow and
lurking other things nameless and dissolving, have not heard
the egret's cry? did not see various the white plumes descend
like downy rests of sleep far fallen from heavier the head so,
questions in a different tongue, built the watery fortress a
citadel of wattles and mortar soon to sink like thought,
a man's no more than that a drowning impulse to move,
forward or back, but in motion hail the great rolling light,
our life, selections from the tenth book of the Bhagavata,
child Krishna off to herd the ruddy kine, into the ocean
of Being we push off from the marshy tract as evening sends
its bright signals in the eastern hemisphere of sky near the
edge where the Pharaohs have their chambers, the ruddy kine
lowing in the dark grass, when will they come home**

**set up the tents, careful to place the papers high,
the girls in pigtails sighing who have lost someone
a song they sing to the end of things,
tie the lantern to the rope, see,
around it gather the fateful moths white winged
buzzing their deadly note, their deadly note,
it is puzzling that we are here, of all places,**

removing our boots, unbuttoning our shirts,
unable to really sleep for the fear,
what is out there just beyond the planet's rim,
***El Trono de los Dioses*   waste land**
like moths to the flame we too,
suddenly speaking and with strange words
as if by a divinity struck, and exchanging
clothes and rags to the wash house wend
in the mind a poesy a blend of literatures
is it far, do we know where
how to sleep in such distress of thought
come to us dream entities bearing paper swords,
a waste land   a land fill   a
sound of huge trucks removing detritus
the sum of history,   off to an ocean
girls in pigtails seen in relief blue bodices
have lost someone   , sighing
we have been to the sacred mountain
to the fogs that curl around the moat
and seen the canopy flapping high over
the sea green pond,   the gazebo
and inside it the statue of the Mother of Heaven
in gowns of transparent azure
but, here, sit ye down
here are cushions of argent threads woven
and the head, lay it to rest   remember nothing,

mysterious this passageway this watery conduit to what
other world, ears ringing the distance it takes to maintain
the mountain, landscape painting, waterfalls of memory a
radiance for a minute, a purity of thought emblems reddening
by day's end winding in and out and through these various canals
flushed with a dying light copper-flecked green baize tinted, overhead
the slow canopy of a late sky sprawls unfurling its alternate
universe of intricate but fading constellations, echoing hours
of remote brass a nostalgia for unwalled cities in the Tuscan past
a forever written backwards in stained apocalyptic mirrors, else
what are these pendants looming in the dusky air these faint

glimmerings assorted jewels pasted to the waning fabric byzantine
elephantine ivory chastened enamel worthy of a dowager empress,
yet through these sluggish shoals we push our errant skiff no compass
to guide the chance voyage into the crenellated night distance,
a sobbing a wary moan childhood whispers somehow come back
to evoke a need for lying down to sleep under the eaves of a forest
hut to dream the black dream of loss beneath leaf piles grown old,
yellow brittle gnarled veins turned to mulch underfoot where
the phantom treads ancient unyielding husk, was a life here a
driven force a

or so it seemed, wandering, could you
never felt so   the thing is,
brilliant flash before my very eyes
the world's skin trembled ever so slightly,
thunder in the nerve green spreading,
a swill shut the pulse, focus lost
tent flapping darkly in the wind
night after, night   however so tender
the first dew felt underfoot, waiting
longing for the transcendent moment
when the driven rain turns to light
such,   someone else was there
before the small portal,   jade in the ear,
husk of time, the ticking
**   pierces the sound barrier**
just outside of   immense, the
how many of us are there in the end,
handful of pronouns, declensions
of substantives according to gender and
number,   we, that is, each to the other,
bound   , and then forgetting who,
and to ask of the deity what, and to
receive, what   , penance on the knees
the canvas flapping wildly now, a sharp
current from mars   , celestial awakening
and to jot down a few lines before,
this is *El Trono de los Dioses*   , high

barely visible just above the mile of dust
encircling the planet,   storm signals
and aftermath of destruction,

inches from the next port, sluggish inert the waterway
wending through mazes of reed and lotus mesh, sticking
the oar into the ooze pushing pushing hard on the pole to move,
and what gives way barely yielding the clayey mud thick
as night on the other side of the moon and switched to darker
where stars barely perceptible and the large hotel abandoned
on the right where ghosts of Chinese rail workers dwell, there
hard by the lightning shattered palm and the totem beasts
howling and prowling through the years of grass and yes
the wasteland the automobile graveyards the diminished
fraction of the world burnt by its ambition, yearning slow
toward the vast and final inch towards, the

III

LEÇONS DE TÉNÈBRES

(a)

not the single nor the plural
but the uncountable near the nexus
of sunset and vine watching the slow
motion of empty cabs drive by in
funereal procession whose mighty death
whose massive stone with just a nick in it
is being conveyed to the lawn of eternal distance
you might say it's the lone ranger or a horse
strapped to the desert of dreams barely
but just barely breathing a reminiscence
like a hotel of forty abandoned floors
filled with dust and the portfolio of air
that belongs to no one any more
standing there for the traffic light to change

for the sky to move its rebus of clouds
to the southwest quadrant where Persephone
waits for a cigarette to begin smoking
the lit end sketching a path for a super nova
isn't it supposed to be by night fall
when the wingèd things begin to stir again
shaping from the vacuum of reality
an evidence of sleep amorphous and pale
and the multiple worlds of light and breath
that constitute for a nano second only
the universe as we think to know it
before falling again wings singed
and tufts burnt into the miasma below
and isn't it at this hour of dusk and aspirin
when the shadows we inhabit start to move
in and out of the map of porous structures
better known as the Fall of Troy
that we commence the journey through
the labyrinth of cocktail love affairs
with its poetry of lipstick and rimmel
etched into the eyes of the walls of heaven
how we flounder in the address and symptom
of something more ancient than this
asking with a bitter accent which is the exit
once we have established a connection
to the cadaverous six-foot doorman
who claims to have known Achilles
before he went down on the south side
in the internecine struggle for turf
it all fades into a present of absinth doors
that elaborate fiction of shuttered windows
memory on trial reduced to embers
& in the dream shrugging off her father's death
bright and effusive as ever her red mane
flashing like a signal in the dark
she moves gracefully eliminating one
by one the lovers she has summered
over the distance of a lifetime

the pomegranate of her mouth
the very music that destroys
even the grass she treads
the minute planets
that thrive on dew
us in their midst

(b)

afterwards in the spacious and elegant lobby of the Mayo clinic
chasing spirit demons out of recently dead bodies
the enormous brass carillon booming in the winter ear
dizzying reflux
                    isn't red the dust of
ancient ascension (s)
                    riddled with flame
the opposing shore its mouth
                    averts the very air
it craves
                    for one I am a thought
sheer crystal ablaze
                    transparency & luster
long rides home to wherever that may be, or is
but doomed however
                    dark the plow
earth underside
                    billows like a flare
arms white as rope
                    head a shock of hair
who hasn't seen once
                    the surface of despair
and renewed the consequences in a greek restaurant
hard by the old catholic mortuary off west center street
you mean the nunnery, the sisters of Saint Mary
in their perennial black ground length robes, frightening
or climbed into the pit
                    to wait out the drug
storm of leaves
                    tension of weir and gas

or is it the rabid arabesques
black saliva sutures
wearing the shore away
the indefinite article
barking the random
ambulances of eternity bearing the circumstantial corpses
back to the dust mound whence all arises, origins
carved in evening air, mephitic, pharaonic coming and going
through 84,00 rebirths to cross the sea of Being
is it then desire
purgatorial wedding feet
soldered bridal veins
gutted husband wear
ink the size of alabaster
a place neither sun nor moon go
head down in the tarmac
angel breathes shattered
dovecote dimension
up the terraced slope climbing twins hand in hand
carving from the snow an incidental paradise
frozen apples the meaning of abracadabra the comic
instantaneous radio fused to a circling search light
coded for something that outdistances memory
when mother can no longer be, and the dog and the ceremony
for a religious assumption and the burning wax tapers
how far to reach
when each blade of grass
is a universe and
children in boxing shorts
fisticuffery in the gloaming
wary in the lunar mansion
to sleep ho heavy head
to pierce the barrier
called the flowers of god
these little imps come roaring through the lobby
knocking down halt lame and healed alike
in the hunt for the magnificent white stag
set loose a hundred years ago and ghosting hills

what fanciful and errant deed
I am sick to the body and dead cry out
nor do the Hounds eat the goslings
but with blood red ears leap into the frosty air
clouds like unto the masters of thought thunder
and the whole earth shudders toppling its peaks
what did the dreamer say then, pray tell
what did indeed the uniform with its gold braid
and strutting like a prince eating cake
rendered silence aloud
reading from the book of Mormon
with wagons still ablaze
crossing the Sioux reserve
pricking their steeds
in ten gallon hats
whooping to declare war
a tornado a mile wide
swept the Zumbro valley
leaving in its wake
nothing standing
waking in a small casket and still dressed in his sky blue
the inch worm and the gallows bird feeding on sweet bread
the way the wind howled around the hotel corner
on the look for a tea house an inn some place for the night
and pointing to the adder shouted "'tis he, milord!"

(c)

into the forest and father chasing shouts "don't go!"
and sweating in the movie house abandoned
remembering the empty medicine cabinet
just wanna find perfection at her Lotus Feet
and the distant shouts from outside either children
or a party in distress the prickling heat and dirty waves
on the lake beach the number of fish belly up silver
heart drained of light life empty of meaning
increasing daily and the distant Indiana steel mills
smoking clogging the air streams with poisons
when Diana Ross and the Supremes were riding high

everything a confusion this is Kali Yuga this is
with waters going every which way and no where
but the boat was veering in the wrong direction
the helmsman drunk and twined in white ivy
whose woods are these what inextricable passage
there were no Blessed Isles no Hesperia nor Arcadia
only the monotony of uncounted days learning
linguistic paraphernalia and laws of phonetic decay
looking for the other side of the eternal edge
can count on none can speak for no one
but keep the girl's name a secret
keep hidden what she said and did and with whom
and hold the lantern away from the doorway
let none seek her for barter or affront
at least for today and the moon's rushing tide
sleeping in the name the unutterable like fireflies
and the planetary monograph destroy it right now
legend and the hierophant of the Olympians
just a stone's throw from the hospital
surrender earthly love of wife child parent
or at the benzene stand which is the entrance to hell
loitering tramps illumined with song to the dawn
escape from the 84,000 rebirths sometimes a goat
go naked eating goop avoiding all mortal contact
sometimes an insect and others a human damned
and above all destroy the wandering remnant
the light above my head the walls ever nearer
how she danced in a red kimono inebriate mad
and let none be the wiser for her who was
and forever the yes in her eyes a darkening
like a spinning top in my brain illusion of her
run into the woods the labyrinthine and cold
memory of the empty medicine cabinet
the rishis the divine ones the mendicants waiting
one by one the days become wingless and blind
we grow old aging in the slanting faltering light
forgetting which is the name which the body
shadows nothing but shadows

whispering

(d)

**does anything make sense any more
tree branches swinging in the wind
how many darknesses must stain the air
how much grass underfoot must be painted
listen to the insects in their archaic worlds
making the rounds among the fallen planets
how summer is this moment of grief unbound
how green this errant must of undue form
hear the muted singing in the leaf
how much its winter pains the silent vein
swirling the mass of remembered thursday hair
reddened in the crater of the missing mind
this is the hospital of dusky mountain passes
this is the lobby where spent childhoods gather
summoning a season in extinct x-rays
chalking sidewalks with a legend of yellow
where is the valley of the water bearer
where is the dale where chanting the shadow
multiplying in its chaotic skirts mourned
celestial deaths raining from the clouds
how little is the house become in its lawn
so lessened by the migrant heron's tune
how fast space reduces the time it takes
to travel from one life to the next
shake the gourd-rattle and darken its tone
speak if you can the flaming distance
what are the shapes of ink when the dream is done
where can anyone go walking at such an autumn pace
you tell me if the face in the mirror is one
or as many as the days it has taken to wake
I am not that one nor the other in its latin
they are writing furiously in the tundra
a long poem about the residue of love
snowflakes turning blue in the absent room
gravel mounting against the aging tide
vedanta of the spotted deer and white roe**

so many things to think about and nothing
books to discard because they are not butterflies
an urgency to dispel myths about alcohol
music arranged like sand in the japanese sleeve
to hear it is to become a devotee of satin
a longing to sleep underneath vermillion
remembering if possible the sexual act
the union of fish and star in the desert
or is to misunderstand everything from the start
taking the text and renumbering it
using a calligraphy of forgotten characters
in long slanting flourishes on the skin
of one who died years ago in san francisco

(e)

bells of dead copper resounding before dawn
sleep's ivory thicket dissolving in black dew

will I know you when the sun shakes its head
over the dappled distant mountains of cathay

switches of russet grass whipping lightly in the air
for a body to draw nigh for blood to rise in welts

what is all but forgotten in this tenuous labyrinth
may well be the mind in its first oriental light

did I tell you to come at the hour of the cricket
did I ever summon you across this bleak distance

to come running through the empty temple
praying to each and every headless deity   AOI

who are rattling the 84,000 spears in the unlit vale
the amassed souls of purgatory hungry for silence

look! in the western quadrants of sky flocks of geese
who spell out the longing for summers of endless grain

had I not looked into the abyss would I have seen the mirror
had I not gone blind would I ever have seen your face

it is the other world you are walking under a great shade
umbrellas elephants staggering with the weight of the sun

it is a far other world you are walking a spirit of shadow
take care not to veer to either side of the highway

where clusters of malignant gods with nets of cancer
lie in wait those half formations of tideless ink baths

what baleful design circling the morning air outshines
setting in relief the horses whose toil doubles by the day

what errant planet what constellation gone dead wrong
marks the minute of our brief and only encounter

did I ever tell you to wear red in that fashion
or to put your hair up like an empress stepping out

the mansion of the moon meant for your dwelling
lies smoking in the nether moor of Etruscan countersigns

and the doorman who announces daily the list of the dying
shifts within the enormous corpus of linguistic decay

oblivious of the rules prescribed by the Sanskrit parrot
and instead pronounces of all names your Name today   AOI

IV

LUNA PARK

it comes as a surprise no it doesn't on
the lakeside silver the bushes burnished

by the last light ever echoing the mirage
of voices tumbling off the ferris wheel
I am not arguing for the full moon
moving like a mysterious lantern in the sky
opposite the unconstructed city that awaits
the innumerable dead who have gathered
around the fallen oak to pray for the mill stone
no surprise that the sparkle of distant flares
imitates the immense reflections of mountains
can it be that the living never cease to breathe
those innumerable dead whom we have known
not as the disappeared but as the engines
of an insane memory we have of living
of having lived on this silver lakeside
burnished with bushes which are mere outlines
the disparate and calumniating members of
of the dense greenery swarming near Luna Park
that casts songs out like rust into the night
the raucous tutti frutti of eternal adolescence
obdurate fickle licensed to embrace all forms
the rushing swoon of consciousness in white
spreading an even whiter shadow into blank
tossed the hair to one side parading vermillion
her tattered skirt and grazed knees barely
visible moving in and through the shrubbery
coupling with the very absences of ego
king and subject alike in the nicotine embrace
that alcohol and smoking have destroyed
the piecemeal bric a brac and nonsense
with a pair of eyes and longing ready to cry
listening for the words of the song to "mean"
cylindrical syntax of the most archaic thought
bucolic grasses vanishing into a mere darker
than the legend of time
bucolic grasses vanishing into a mere darker
than the legend of time
cylindrical syntax of the most archaic thought
impostors the dead because they reappear

in dreams mocking cajoling spitting in their
brandnew store bought clothes creased pants
pomaded hair skirts of flourishing pleats
multicolored hair pieces jissom streaked cheeks
the whole paraphernalia about immortality
riding the roller coaster at Luna Park subdivided
by immense extra planetary trajectories lies
about the history of this and that plunging
necklines waistbands of Siamese rubber golden
temples acrostics with the names of the infernal
did we never return home that night in May?
and insist on non-existing rights to formulate
libraries with volumes of cuneiform imprints
dusty rolls of endless text in neo sumerian latin
diacritics like moonspells and iota glosses removed
from the margins and the never ending poem
heroes strangled in their hexameters and Lo!
queen Dido or someone like her bound and gagged
in the classroom chalk smeared and sobbing
the race to the blackboard to conjugate irregular
verbs and the missing pronouns of pornography
the skilled letter head that declaims justice
for the black man in Arabia just south of Hyde Park
you may not recognize these enormous poesies
am I to understand the intricate details of sleep
merely by posing as a sand man on the viaduct
that leads from Mount Ida in Crete to the cataracts
of the upper Nile oh how tired the mind becomes
the visceral extrapolation of thought and memory
disjunct issues of time and space on the grassy slope
was this the victory you employed the parallel bars
the succinct invocation to the gods of soil and grit
oh let us please this is not the way the uninformed
the practice of self mutilation of genital immobility
by the shores of Silver Lake littoral transduction
of polyphemic verses ululated at high frequency
and on mars they are painting the water red
isn't it queer how we fall apart by the water's edge

and on venus mercurochrome dunes and silt
dissolve in a flood of italics and infra-red waves
intrinsic details of that *why didn't you call me*
night stars falling and cluster bombs in the ears'
windows what a charade it was, joe,
are we spent with all our planning for hope's
isoglosses you wouldn't tell I didn't ask
dialing leaf after leaf trying to get in touch
this *battibecco* a surfeit of color schemes a wind
with the inner Diana a plague on arrows & stones
a fling's watch away from christ's mass the narrow
colder misery we never owned and the old chevvy
blackening in the gravel put-put exhaust fumes
go to my head and see stars at high noon swinging
invisible rotations of the whet stone in the garage
odor of benzene and old whiskey the fishing poles
like markers of an irregular destiny hanging
from the timbered ceiling if gramps ever knew
the evening was crystal clear with the Pleiades'
excess fires lighting up the whole eastern hemisphere
I will go flying with you tonight we'll ride the monorail
all the way to downtown wherever and go shopping
for muskets leather sashes corsets figure-8 shoe laces
the gamut of domestics to bewitch and destroy
multiply the times I disowned you by the moon tide
flying with you tonight to the seven celestial mansions
cushioning with velvet your padded cell Oh One!
I'm not getting older *I am old* 'neath the spreading willow
without you I am ceasing to be much easier going
solo driving this dream machine into the tundra
a hundred light years per hour

BIGGA BUKKA NO HAKKA

how can I wake behind such reveries looking through
the owl glass into the till where hands forage for romance
in a sub alpine dialect locking ringlets darkly silent
each finger poised to indicate the persona offuscata
marginally taciturn holding the mask upright
but pertaining to the eyes mascara and rimmel drip

-ping! 's alarms going off in the pillow already
how is to sleeve sleep's off draining drink's seep
ho-ho heavy head's lead tantrum pushing dank a
dust bowl framed in gilt spectacle what a sight you
was holding up Orion's belt in the left hank whilst
reciting in the right angular a dialogue of all sadness
to be even as the road unwinds through autumn mulch
misty listing shorewards in a daft sort of cycle Arthurian
in meter and feet counting long syllables twice
put your ankle shift forward and hold the pulse so's
I can take a better loose at you moon-weft and all
it's hard to drink this much tonight I'm already insane
buckled to this beer shaft looking for my advance ticket
to the big tent a show for all reasons white puff
ancient leggings greaves hasps winches shields a shift
at a time loping through the grazing zone wreck in sight
when who's do I see but the sound-alike version of
Romeo falling off his ladder with no net below
cabloom! picked up his brains with a scooper
and divested the shadow of its glowing raiment
don't that make for a tragical thing all down sided
so happens nightly we were sailing along using
clear water for a mirror when all we could see
was and ever will be the thrift of a thousand million stars
caught in the mesh of aqueous thought I dizzied
at the mere idea of you down below sinking surface
of a countenance no god would take back limp
as the blanket mother poured over us the night we
drunk as two angels off the leash fell up the stairs
arm in arm necking whitely oft as winsome could
how vast was my empire! what year was it 496?
reciting the pandects decoding the effluvia byzantine
aghast at the ruin in the bedroom vomit and maps
spread across the ancient persian rug of Alcibiades
then sat we down and talked 'til dawn of great poetry
citing Sappho and Catullus and the hoary lyric tradition
and bucolics and eclogues too and waves came over us
sweeping us into the mass of watery drownings sung

by bards and troubadours alike to this day, amen!

what? that was the fireworks night by Silver Lake
everyone was running to and fro blinded by the spectacular
and the barkers at the gate to Luna Park bustling striped
with faces like plastered rhododendrons didn't you think
it did not take forever to die it just happened so fast
when you weren't even looking that way the dusty trail
facing the immemorial Tao the masters playing bamboo flutes
careful never to speak rolling eyes back into the centuries
the beautiful lonesome sound reedy and whispering
in the hills it is in the dun colored distant hills which
we never did reach thinking it once an easy journey
over pack saddle and livery hose and everything jangling
asterisks the hard edge of each paragraph near the south
took your shoes off someone did and left you for dumb
frosted the soles of your feet as you ran unconscious
through the city whose map you had just completed
yellow borders hyphenated trunk lines canals rusty barges
this is what I get for reading too much for comparing
my self to the canonized who "knew" for drinking dark
the already spent allusion to the gates of heaven AOI

forgetting is not so easy soft the pigeons speak shhh
dawn the great aubade I sing, joe   hearest not?

V

AUBADE

"Lanqand li jorn son lonc en mai"
Jaufré Rudel

silver lid inside out
-hiscent ouverture   unfurled
                    light!
rolling dark masses heaving westward

from far below the moiling millions
the faceless sleepers in their mattresses
of grit and turmoil groaning dream spent
harsh the lot meted them to play out the day
on some asiatic shore   spear smitten
or to be bidden by some atavistic god
one with squinting eyes and tripe hanging out
to perform some unspoken deed darkening
windows the hasp of a ghost ship
waves pounding loud against the pane
wake!   shrill gull skreeks circling above
flurry of wings grayish mists unwinding
forth then do we unplanned send the mind
amongst the flower beds of antiquity
to choose its destiny   as if there were a choice
a sudden turn in the spare becoming
of still another life   splash!

when they had departed from the island without Herakles,
bereft on account of his beloved Hylas, with heavy heart
they pushed on through the watery main, intent on pursuing
their cursed destiny, knowing full well which gods had a grudge
and which ones to propitiate, hands locked to the oars and eyes
pinned on the stars above to guide them

gathered up flowers from the yards
blowing a fine yellow powder   calling out names
long since forgotten   *"Hylas!"*
each in their sleep a different man
each on waking a distant cousin to none
palms chafed raw from rowing
wind chewed the ropes swung
uselessly and the brine eating their skin
seemed to come alive crawling
up as far as the cheek bone
just below the twitching eye pulse
how to regain strength enough to defy
the goddess whose totem bird

grey–eyed mottled
rests mockingly on the prow
how to sprout wings
like the soul to fly against the heat
smoking cigarette after cigarette
dense and damp faint flares
blowing red in the sultry cabin
telling yarns about days in Mycene
wearing gold masks
having a go at the rutting queen
'morn sparkling like emerald
wagons hitched up
to pairs of milk white oxen
skull craving and crazy like fly swarms
for the hour to spread its dazzle into
sound of the mast cracking
Fortune's turbulent sprays whipping
the foul and misty atmosphere
siren song distance
when would they ever again

it was summer 1956 when everything seemed to end
when everything seemed to begin in the fine sheets of dew
sprinkled over the folding fields and groves by Mayowood,
like a casket the future hove into view with its horses lathered
sleek and black chomping at the bit, a girl named Sharon Dee Crawly
riding on the back seat of a convertible driving down Broadway
around midnight shouting out your name, your name Ivan,
the wake of things the multiversed unconscious of root leaf
blade and vine spanning the inch of mind where red augments
at the speed of light and the dream of living and dying takes on
the elements of the kaleidoscope and you are and you are not
lying next to her in a darkened room listening to Elvis Presley
hauntingly moan Blue Moon

then the corn ripened tall in the southern field
and the months too many to be numbered
flew as on the wings of a dragonfly iridescent

and face down as if peering into Hades
the eventual hero of his own dream spell vomited
wonders of Tenochtitlan just glimpsed!
there he saw dimension after dimension peel
away like onion skin and the Whole shine forth
neither to the right nor to the left of the Axis
but in the troubling diameter of the Myrmidons
millimeters below the pyramid of the Sun
a black flame shot out
was it envy ire guilt sloth pride ***shine forth***
lust avarice overweening hybris ***shine forth***
in a pink button-down collar shirt and ivy league tie
and in Teotuhuacan both splendid and ruinous
under the black Aztec sun
"tous les matins du monde"
and emerging as if from a shed snake skin
his intelligence that the cosmos encompassed
skimming constellations born and not yet born
with the ease of a
a black flame shot out
was it just ego?
millimeters below the pyramid of the Moon
and when the autumn winds began to blow chill
dry husks rattling in the dim yellow air
and the months too few to be remembered
passed as dirty raindrops on a speeding window
the former hero of his other dream face down
lay oblivious of the netherworld under him
the splendid mansions where the Pharaohs go
when they have had enough of the light

"… he was a noble man, prince of Blaia, fell in love with the countess of Tripoli, sight unseen, for the good that he had heard about her from the pilgrims come from Antioch, and of her wrote many verses with fine melody and meager words, and for a desire to see her he joined the crusades and put off to sea, and on the ship fell ill, and was brought to Tripoli to an inn, dying, and

when the countess heard of this she came to him, to
his bed taking him in her arms, and he knew it was the
countess, and momentarily recovered hearing and sense
of smell, and praised God, who had kept him alive long
enough to see her, and so he died in her arms, and with great
honor she had him buried in the house of the Temple,
and on that day she became a nun for grief that she had
of his death."
what was Enkidu to do?

that was the morning I took off with Joel Pugh
hitchhiking to Fort Snelling and Minnehaha Falls
to study speech organization and linguistic change
once the great unknown explored by *père* Hennepin
alarm of the chattering jay birch bark canoes sliding
stealthily into limpid waters under watchful father Sunne
pathology of phonetic decay twelve types of aphasia
wheel keep on burning
"si che gran pianto e cruccio fu in Troia"
was there ever a morning so bright with promise
what magical world sparkled out of the asphalt ribbon
highway 52 Oronoco Pine Island Zumbrota Cannon Falls
on either side old Ojibway legend wove spider webs
that crystallized forever sky's intricate azure
thumbs out standing defiantly on the road side
humming and whizzing vehicles full of gods tearing past
the occasional deity with heart stopping to pick us up
for a lonesome stretch with hand painted decorations
of green ivy gnome woods fishermen gone daft
illusory villages of teepee and cobalt drifting lazily
because there is no limit to memory because
teeter totter clouds brilliant array of enigma and ink
splashing down on the man built urban horizon
highlighted by stockyards state capitol university dorms
Joel nervously self confident already future spent
at my side jiving at the benzedrine driven truckers
who manned the wheel effortlessly asleep in the light
grand pantomime of life! on the city streets high

with the poetry of ecstasy and jubilant sexuality
which way to turn what road to take dreaming
whose big shadow to follow into the numbing wake
that destroys all who plunge into the galactic mirage
Joel ticking off the minutes left of his stay on earth
grinning like a medicine man who can't keep a secret
performing the supreme blues number of his adolescence
and talking fast to trees clap-board houses girls all
declaring his red-topped presence to the cosmos
whiplashed to the racing metal that too quickly darkens
coming home that afternoon bathed in a luminescence
that only night can project we start with amaze
as the radio explodes with a wild electric guitar
and a hillbilly guy singing Be-Bop-a-Lula

"che 'l chiaro giorno fu tornato bruno"

> ***"Those Dawns even now equally***
> ***the same of unchanged color,***
> ***move on; concealing the black***
> ***monster, bright with gleaming***
> ***forms, brilliant beaming."***
> ***Vedic hymn to Dawn***

forthy ferny foot 'neath the scapular graze
unpen the ruddy kine flush from dark welkin
hush blank 'chens histed lissome behind walls
patent glaze an eye a single glassy doth amaze
circling the dance 'tween reed and flame air
lit up hastening to become more than itself
the gleaming forms equally of mottled hue
unchanged color dash streak the rubescent
orb climbing into the third heaven mercurial
shining of brilliant beaming chased as emerald
or dew designed on the patient and blind leaf
doth then the monster black stir in mind's lair
removed from sleep the doleful as day puts on
some flashy flair mushrooming clouds hugely

oriental dashed with orange tapioca verdigris
asterisms hunt the belt of tears charging dark
into the first Hour's topaz greek unhinged doors
through which rush frothing the steel sleek steeds
hooves clanging on the ionosphere's metal canopy
like lightning bolts their nostrils breathing flare
fixing from one invisibility to the next the flame
eternal the massy redundancy of time's events
concealed the black monster starts the daily tour
shifts of red in slattern ranks th'ooze primordial
from which all that live repeatedly awake alas
doze full recriminations of violated dreams aware
on lawns empty out the dumped thought confusion
concocted betimes by the guile of master Negative
and but then do we consider the universe to turn
high above fused to Dawn's pearly weft swirling
the immutability of hue and tone the loud freesong
like some infinite violin string descending ever
to where dust has its origins the yellow maze & flux
dense the dusky whorls released by chafing deities
upturned and overruled by the Monster's negritude
+++
there it is, Aubade
do then glistening go and sing
to the evanescent dews the rites of spring
wake then Love, the tender

VI

CARCEL DE AMOR

"voi mi tenete e sempre mi terrete
occhi miei bei, nell'amorosa rete"
Boccaccio, Filostrato

primera parte

the time when Parvati smeared herself
with red sandal-paste ***no tengo palabra de nadie***
todo se disuelve **mountain peak**
to mountain peak in the flaring mists
painting the air with memory
eons since the last encounter with the Big God
her thighs all a tremble and the left eyelid
quivering as if for a bad omen ***ni sé porque***
nadie me recuerda **waterfalls**
rushing out of the morning sky
you know why and litters with yellow the vast unknown
pebbles sparkling like mica 'neath her feet
and starshine glow in the depth of her eyes
"lemme go, Lover" hoarse shouting
the metaphysical tattoos of the amorous bout
light years ago with ShivJi still raw
shivers up and down the spine
into how many dictionaries
has she divided her life
ni yo tampoco recuerdo
a nadie
flashes of imperial lightning bright green
hailstones rampant floods life gone amok
followed by what is the longest and saddest
looking but not finding
when she was just a little bitty and skin was
one rosy song softer than
and the grasses underneath hymned the universe of
her footprints **well wasn't that a time**
all bells and silver clouds ***lágrimas sueltas***
corriendo para nadie
clad in her pink finery
cutting a figure between rock and mountain cave
alluring elusive mysterious enigmatic haunting
the wind shaping the vault of her enormous hair
and everywhere the billows and chime rhyming
her name that no one can hear

underchosies
and silk stockings argent sprinkled glittering
for all the morning to wake
looking for a love
labios pintados bermejo
cuchicheando en la oreja de nadie
checking for all the diacritics
tossed into the empyrean glimmering asterisks
wasn't her the Himalayan sweetums the
whatcha call the dancing fling her shapely
ever in downsized ivory and chemise see through
pellucid shimmering wavering quivers
a thrill to see "the" her coming and going peekaboo
nightless frump where was that love
looking for in abstract ashcan paintings
in sparkle-all tease-me dust rags
like millennial cloud-swarms mounting jewels
of light in the preterit beyond of time
the quintessential the acme and apex
worn like the crown of red too far to reach
above her glistening sand-papered brow
ah her deliquescence her evanescence
her her her what! ***ojos sin blanco***
percibiendo la nada de nadie
pepper-rican heat served up in a boiling can
Uma half woman half you name it
all but naked strumping in teeter-totter heels
up the shady residential street the slattern dump
the hoyden primped to kill
looking for true love
any love at all in fact her hair peroxide orange
her lips my god the size and flame of them
that would floor Catullus ***basia mille***
into perpetuity and the death of all eternity
nights without count the supreme annihilation
of love the one and only
jujube voodoo hex in a torn skirt
helium voiced chanting some gaga number

as if she meant It ***olvídame no me dejes***
con nadie
errant Parvati disheveled tongue loose
barking woof woof like the animal she is
inimitable of orgasm the endless
ululating mercilessly longing
for hoary old shaggy ShivJi
still doing his dance of destruction
way on top of the world
as we know it
knocking everything to smithereens
splitting the atom for the nth time
bathing Parvati in her supreme distance
with the billion watt light of Love
origin and end of the universe AOI

segunda parte
"to die of not being able to die"
thus Teresa de Ávila pierced
to the quick by the marble lance of
and Hari took as many wives as pleased
love of the formless god who in turn
like a dog ate bread from Namdev's hand
on all fours a bag of stones on her back
forsaken by the blue-faced god Radha
built in her name a temple and danced
naked the *gopis* emerged from the water
shouting in piercing voices either *Ram* or *Sita*
in a living room on the upper West Side
Mira Bai considered divinely mad
betrothed to the only man in the universe
sat on the divan patiently assailed
by anthropologist and linguist alike
arguably centered in Mathura the mandir
beside the sluggish Jamuna the cowherds
companions to the child-god dreamed
did the Christ himself not wash her feet
the Maudlin red-haired gypsy thing

lingering toward evening to hear the lowing
gentle dust clouds melancholy sunset
in the Maghreb where the muezzin drowns
his final prayer eyes rolled back
who has not seen from within the Love
traversed the Ocean of Being and drowned
reanimated a cow brought the river
from its dry bed turned the temple around
careful not to step on the slightest living
the weaver Kabir who met Namdev
and Goraknath and Guru Nanak
do we not all praise Ahuramazda
does not the element of fire in us all
made vows to be true to One only
slept on stone slabs imitating Lions
sufis dancing wild gyres around the
and great shadows of night encroaching
and the Stone in the midst of nowhere
worshipped deities with skull-garlands
soles of the feet painted colors of heaven
indigo to mercurochrome blanched ivy
in between calls for Jihad the Adoration
bhakti Vedanta with its small white deer
in the annunziata position not being able
to die *how can we obtain the highest sphere*
crowded into a hot vehicle to cross the frontier
Nuestra Señora de Guadalupe on the dashboard
"Borderline, I'm gonna lose my mind"
++++++++++++++++++++++++++++++++++++
I cut the hair of my mirror self
counting forward the years remaining
the lessons left to learn in the grammars
the loves left to remember and recount
as are leaves like the accounting of man
budding verdant to be torn wither or fall
inclement seasons music that cannot be heard
a face from the mist emerging and insects
in the faint ear buzzing or whirring

toward the flame drawn into darkness
the eternal insentient plain *todos morimos*
***huérfanos* however indistinct a face emerges**
the years remaining cutting the mirror self
hair growing verdant budding as years
of men are recounting leaves wither
falling from the branch to be torn crying
a bleeding voice out of grammars
seasons conjugated like irregular verbs
of rain and sleet and hail to be heard
like insects whirring chirring in the faint
grasses too mown drawn to darkness
ear listening to the *todos morimos*
forward loves remaining in mirror
of selves counting however indistinct
a voice emerging a face complex as
drawn to darkness the insentient plain
lessons left to bud like greening insects
faintly the ear falling as are the branches
of men drawn to a complex face emerging
***huérfanos* cutting the hair in Borderline**
toward the drawing flame emerging faint
an ear left to learn accounting the grammars
left to be heard a music the eternal crying
wither and buzzing fall bleeding leaves
as are the voices of man recounting loves
lost or drawn forward as are remaining
the insects in darkness drawn to grasses
as are mown the hair in the mirror self
emerging faint the face crying indistinct
however complex are drawn flaming
to the bud of seasons raining *morimos*
of my mirror self is there any other?
like irregular verbs the hails and sleet
mist emerging from a face faintly complex
as are the budding of man the music
of loves the accounting like *huérfanos*
that cannot be heard falling the insentient

eternal the hair cutting like irregular
verbs drawn to love and *todos morimos*
whirring chirring darkness the emerging
however indistinct flame cutting like
"to die of not being able to die"
"Borderline, I'm gonna lose my mind"

tercera parte

in the clinic where they treat the wounds of love
Haroun er-Rashid dazed or stoned
looking for the Ka'aba in the middle of Hollywood
prince of Cupids darts him another fling
falls unconscious whirling dervish in Buick 88
racing the pyramids of thought to their source
whirlpools of deep and incendiary Eyes
jazz frictions in the deep middle of the Unknown
his quiver wavers solemnly sounding the down below
never waking from the thunder and spotted grief
a drum on the equator a lyre somewhere in the Gulf
how dreaming swells the tide's distant rushing
drawing from the moon her deliquescent combs
and sands of voices alarming fill the blowing sleeves
for never again the kiss to touch Her timeless lips
did never then a stone confound the books of algebra
his library tomb a trip through leaves of ink
how drowning fair caliphate the waves return a deer
grazing on the mind's other side so once long ago
a poem inscribed in the grasses of the Mountain
a lyric sung through the flowing princess hair
Jesus wasn't that a swoon the ancient dark
of extra-planetary night the walking tom-tom sticks
each desert the shadow crosses each reddening vine
the ivy round his temples burns a love supreme
and Legend in her course of days inspires
the rudiment of white that gives sleep its size
enlarging the photo of the One with jasmine scent
and powders of the crescent fane abandoned

beside the chinese path leading inward to the heart
how far from light the crumpled form in its abyss
how remote the sound of the tinfoil breath
circling ever more faintly the Beatrice of youth
reducing the promontory where lovers hang
with deathless wish to increase the inch
while surrendering to the weight their sighs
this is long to tell the bridge that crosses space
the zigzag pronoun employed to fake the brain
uttering with simplicity the complex consonants
the undecoded mantra of the venereal jewel
So breathe deeply fragrances of sandalwood and thyme
become conjoined to the sublime Other
speeding in your Buick 88 of flame and metal
pay no heed to the sun's great errors
nor to the lunar rains that fall forty floors
you are become the Elemental undivided
spore within the rock seed in blowing air
yet you have never met her nor once seen her
who dwells in the paradise of screens and shades
who languishes in sheets of archaic vowels
sleeping the remote drugs of ruined Carthage and Troy
never beheld her in the bath of liquid phosphors
her skin the music of alcoholic troubadours
how can the never been assume her idiomatic shape
resolving labyrinths of instamatic reconditioning
even as the Sultan's curtains descend silently
and the hushed amphitheater turns to hematite
the audience of volcanic ash no memory retains
and soundless hands applaud the inky spire
the dialogue between When and Now

"I begin to boil using the force of my thumb
to move heaven from its colors, and when night
with its unspoken trees descends taking me from
the seething waters and the half of me which is
female turns to red coral, then I aspire to the top
the half of me that is corrupted and rust, the male,

I inform light of its incidence and evanescence and
like a rushing wind in the marsh reeds take shape,
while the woman who is in me, the very essence of
me, dissolves becoming liquid the dashing waves
impelled by the moon's white turbulence, against
rock and tower toppling all substance and matter,
there is nothing left but the void, breathing is difficult
and sleeping in stone the vast unconscious beneath,
what am I then, and I am walking down the street
furious to have her the half of me that is inaccessibly
woman, the painted hemisphere of a sky that exists
outside of stone, of the void where the unconscious
dwells swarming with insect galaxies red yellow and
indigo beyond the spectra, the her *who is all of me*
obsessed with her every being in the shimmering
distance of light years of an honorific pronoun
whose use is forbidden, more difficult than ever
to breathe using my index finger to push against
the pharaonic membrane, the her *who is insubstantial*
and whole the all of me that I cannot have behind
the mirror my mother invented at birth, stone and
dense bottomless nothing, and I go sleeping down
the street insane to have a go at her who has consumed
me with obsession, dancing with her in the gutter
singing with her in the back alley strumming with
her in the land fill, how can we be halves of one another,
each is the irretrievable other *unconditionally azure*
circling the mystic tree where our wet clothes hang,
she is the other me the Eleusinian baffle in pony tail
and pink wag and doing a threnody to send the chill,
she must be me all the time when I am not there and
yet I cannot have her until she is all of me, staring dumb
out of a glossy magazine cover some thirty years ago
when like a tempest her hair captured me caught
me in its peroxide mesh and flung me to the seas
where to this day I seethe reaching boiling point and
beyond , the ineffable red at the origin of things
me her what who that art Thou!"

Friend, you have come to the labyrinth

Earth   Air   Fire   Water

whirlpools of deep and incendiary Eyes

VII

TROBAR CLUS

"Quant l'aura doussa s'amarzis"
Cercamon

a)

"the trips's not over yet!!!"
hungry ghosts writing from down under
a message years in the taking
and the leaf falls from the bough
some days so bad *you can never have it back*
the wind lays the grass down low
you wake from the siesta *knowing it's over*
a dream all it ever was a painted
air passing over a nothing earth a
shake it out of the photo if you can
dismount it hide it behind the unread books
a summer like that smoke inside the glass
the sheer impalpability of it *ashes in no time flat*
I ain't coming home no more I ain't
possessed by immaterial reflections of mind
bent over the water the pliant willow
distance of hills dun colored dusky
where myth keeps its kings of yore
remoteness of the door *can never forgot that*
purgatory of the unlit basement
or sunny afternoons when you undressed
the shadow and its poignant shoe

and in the sky thought to see your uncle's
phantom fighter plane streak by
it was what was beside you lying there
it was that brother lying there
husk of breathing just like you your half
intuit everything that was to be
how is it we are dead already in that wan light
what purpose do we serve wending
aimlessly through soldiers' field *a cold whisper*
to write a poem about some eyes
or draw night from the corner house the pines
did no one ever come back from it
and in the alley way fling gravel stones
against tin cans and echo the unknown
now that *he is gone* I am more than ever he
I mirror his eyes his nose his lips
I grow into the ravel of untended thoughts
the mass of nerves *the undigested brow*
or waiting on the curbstone for the dog
to come running with the paper
is that me around the bend in faded t-shirt
the canvas of life yet to be consumed
a friday night symposium of beer and cigarettes
songs that riddle words that never mean
a joe a bro' a postcard from *the nether world*
who can answer the unbidden phone
who can order from the restaurant of the Greeks
the lofty order *that brought Achilles down*
or is that my brother round the bend in faded
what is skin that it cannot be peeled
or hair unkempt and the drunk on the stairs
what is the small verse *lhude sing cucu*
which exactly is the window that spares night
and of the myriads of stars blazing
which is the one where we linger our summer
intent on a single blade of grass
a half-heard word an insect sounding its viol
the bicycle leaning against the fence

irruption of red from the solar flares
that blind us and *we lose our selves*
walking into the library of darkness to look for
the volume of the alternate dimension
pictures we share in the multiple hour
of nothing but *sand and emptiness*
alone the two of us in the children's corner
fantasizing a medieval warp
black lozenges of time and space *pyramids!*
is this the access to grief
is this the shutter that precludes light
or we are climbing Plummer Hill
searching for the cave *of abandonment*
sure that the music we hear comes
from the brooks and dragonflies of *loss*
when the faerie realm was bright
but longing the ancient wound the bitter *knowing*
us embrace the unfolding
map of lawns in the act of invention talking
to one another in the attic *heat*
pretense of *flight* and the angelic hosts
legend of becoming so much *other*
than the ones in the small and fading photos
to paint a *sea* upon the bedroom wall
a water so immense neither of us could perfectly drown
glyphs of rain and impending stone
cold premonitions falling asleep one last time
"the trips's not over yet!!!"

b)

grains of sand running down
blades of grass now finite in number
the causeway to the heavens less steady than before
the hollyhocks priceless in color now a fading
memory wind-bent beside the white washed garage
within tents of fantastically braided upholstery
upwards of tens of millions of cities clamorous and ruined

and the 16,100 brides of Krishna married in a day
do we wend eastwards in caravanserais ten thousand leagues
passing the furiously rent dreams of the surrealists
who walk cosmically sleeping in the enormous eiderdown
which are the mansions of thunder and silence
how impossible a single childhood split in half
sitting on freshly painted folding chairs the length of ink
and we speak to the artists who have gone divinely mad
and we talk to them of the fables of number and order
the rank divisions of countless dead still moving among us
of dictators in phalanxes of quill and lapis lazuli
spitting into the face of the Daimon who invented them
and we converse with them about the infinite afternoon
in the atelier of Gog and Magog spinning whirligigs of Love
absence of all but the last 13 billion years of time
and when someone calls our names do we really know which
is the Name and which the shadow of the name
it is heat and the profusion of sky bursting with ether
balloons of incorporeal stigma and hues and tones
like rivers racing backwards into the dust of things
if they present us with books and poems and science
if they award us with the gifts we cannot understand
and we shake their invisible hands and congratulate them
for having visited us in all this summer of intense yellow
do they tell us to go back westwards to the limbs
to the subterfuge of grass and waving corn below painted awnings
or do they only tell us to just sit a while longer
for the cool of the evening with asterisks and grammars of light
can we ever be ourselves again in that dappled hour
watching the lizard immobile in its eternity of two minutes
listening intently for the song of the leaf turning brown
shall we once more amble lazily south of the great highway
to the water with its sands of immensity and longing
casting shadows among the foliage of historical anomalies
being uncertain who it is chattering in the shifting branches
and we speak to the artists who have gone divinely mad
for it is to ourselves we address these innumerable topics
counting down the decline of the west with its european mind

our fingers search for clues in the unmown grasses
lawns of sudden night spring up where we wander half and half
the improbable hotels of the heavens light up in a blaze
both terrible and instantaneous and just as suddenly disappear
somewhere in the galaxies of cuneiform and devanagari
that go gravitating centrifugally out of our heads into the unknown
a blaze like never before this moment when both ourselves
and not ourselves we revel in the pointillistic blindness of the pharaohs
dipping our feet into the passing stream with its minute civilizations
of midge and eel and dragonfly we become with them Unconscious
do we somehow return home to our beds below the tattooed sea
does mother put a hand upon our fevered brows and sing a chant
is it nirvana we have been to and back in a matter of instants
is it to create to make grow the person from within to blossom
darkly in the insane refulgence we so deeply intuit
becoming one another in the swarming *Transformative Vision*
is it as we fall finally sick to remember just once
hollyhocks like fragile heads bent against a whitewashed garage

c)

who will surrender first the wounded text
radiating a thunder of afternoons without appeal
hail and grass in ruins the immense omen of eternity
shadows working themselves across absent lawns
and among them a messenger breathless who asks
which of you two is Maheshvara?
are we not both the divine introspection of matter
the fleeting coruscations of stellar drift caught
in the play of a forgotten birthday party
to celebrate the spectacular and annual Routine
which is the reminiscence of the moment in Oblivion
when submerged in the amniotic tide we signaled
to one another with the language of unborn fingers
a poetry of insane recognitions and speculations
mutilated ciphers and dendra of time unannounced
our birthright the moment we hit the light of day
winters away from the awakened mind of understanding

there is nothing beside the wattle hut
and even less beneath the shattered palm
whose fan is waving hard by the rock
what shoe is missing in the plundered mulch

what is ancient lorn fragmented apart
what is thickened by smoke and dusk
inches from the place we first met
miles from the home we never had

a suchness of waves enormous and sweet
hunkered down over a diminishing pearl
can ever the blind so hardly see
dumb flashing thunderheads aloft

where's to go what's to think and why
summer's one day left and greening
somber shades didn't they shift
memory's crystalline remains ablaze

who was it among the two of us
waiting on the curb for the maps
unfolding in their own true sky
to first name the roadside accident

head back on the blissful grass
watching keen eyed for heaven's epic
writ big by changing clouds to espy
drowsy drifting like fleeting insects

I have immemorial longing to rest beside
you on the sleepy banks of the Zumbro
and though the tip of my penis is burning
to lie wherever your ashes are strewn

nothing else makes sense nor the songs
of the troubadours in that old blue book

nor the loom of language nor the house
mysteriously poised on the edge of time

where we thought the riddles of distance
or the simple efforts of the pharaohs to die
took place in an elaborate silence of honeycombs
where like detectives we looked for clues

to lie beside you of a stifling afternoon
on our stomachs on the baked cement
beside the swimming pool's drowning
voices the sun taking us in its red vortex

to never move again in this siesta
filled with the humming of ancient stars
and the cyclical road trips of galaxies
immuring us in the hour of dead heat

next to your corpse hands folded flowers
eyes rose water lapels sandalwood incense
taking your breath for mine deeply
the endlessness of a rhyme in *trobar clus*

VIII

DARK MATTER

when will planet earth collide with its nemesis
when the Achaeans quit drawing water from the well
and the oracle ceases chewing the bitter laurel leaf
it isn't because we found carbonized on a tractor
some distance from town a pair of incinerated angels
nor that on our return from the moon that night in may
singing countless rounds of the hymn to Demeter
that we suddenly forgot precisely who we were
descending through miles of sleep into a sandy cove

spears in hand immediately alert to the death at large
some immense shadow beast lying in wait on the rock
beside the roaring instance of darkening waves
nor seared by the hallucinations of Saint Adolf II
"Ynaventura! Great empress of Bengala of the 28 celestial lights!"
supreme and elegant grace of spiritism and et cetera
are we by any means transported from the doggerel of fear
but by laying sacrifices to the One or the Other goddess
who has benignly brought us home from the hospital
and swaddled us in the raiment of long gone heroes
then by some hap do we begin to experience the light
withdrawn from the mean quarters of high school
and ragged with the excitement of new found grammars
heights we then perceive talking rapidly to mirrors
to the glass objects placed in our hands in place of weapons
what a depth opens up what profound ecstasies
do we ken the errors of the sun the multiple circuits
round and about the ninth heaven and the *thirteen deity*
descending by rope of fire and stone to other childhoods
to the mass of unformed myth waiting to be remembered
and I am not with but am YOU brother in the Descent
pyramids inverted by sheer excess of shadow exult!
stowaways of illusion and contour we watch art unfold
unyielding precipices of the most massive delusion
we mark the quotations of the Vishnu avatars unholy
in the reconsidered round dance of trembling adulteresses
all adoration and devotion in their dovecote of madness
earrings upside down necklaces around the ankles
great pearls of white sweat lapsed on to their fevered faces
they are Ours for the taking clasped to the recondite
and hugely red mysteriously chanting in an archaic Aztec
foot-stomping with eagle feathers in their hands Loud
how is it this is only happening in the ninth grade
and we are just come back from the Mysteries of Delos
necking with girlfriends on Lee Ann Meyer's porch
lit up by the universe of fireflies and lunar moths
octaves of a celestial music and as many decades later
the swooning night sky comes to take one of us away

purplish cloud formations like sculpted arhats
dust bowls swirling in fiery dislocations of thought
to be counted among those who read the Decline
and seriously considered Gauguin or Matisse to be
seers of the present condition that of fevered mitochondria
the push and pull of progress leaping steel high vaults
into the integers of systems too rapid to be assimilated
can the sky be ever so forlorn ever so sideways tilting
in its levered yellows and crenellated disparate arches
how did we come to know this abyss of monopolistic terror
byways obsessed by crows and the leaf-eating caterpillar
we amble outwards from the archipelago of heat
observing in their infinite transience the souls of metal
and are caught unawares by the Instant of eternity
the singular minute when the finger goes lost in grass
and evening comes rushing in with its vials of ether
to prepare the house with its multiple beds and hearths
the multifaceted association of hair and Beauty
is slipped between the dream's paper-thin layers
so that waking with new fingers and a digest of green
we can turn the monograph of air page by page
and read star script in large hues of hematite and rust
where it clearly says DIVINE CHAOS burning loam
terrestrial labyrinth the adolescence you have earned
blurring all words into the One in libraries of light
turned inwards your animus and anima take flight
terrific the threnody that lays Achilles to rest
and the tears of the Muses pour like flames into glass
everywhere the tale is the same and of a great disorder
confounding ritual and mask in a forest of lies
each takes the other by the waist and bends downwards
into the lair where Persephone mourns the seasons
perpetual blossoming of thorn-apple and dogwood
and when they bestow the Eglantine on us for the Poem
we have been constantly writing and destroying
we can but strut the stage blindly with a mantic fusion
that conjoins ether to the heraclitean flame of origins
alcohol in abundance and the root that blackens love

vessels of impermanence the human kind lists longing
for shores ever more remote beyond reach lost in mists
to hear the cries of the drowning in the bile-green deep
you ask how does each thing name its own confusion
what is the dark matter of Transformation being born
signaling from mountain peaks to the Goddess who reviles
and everything starts and ends at the self same nexus
dizzying interpolations of syntax and putrefactions
it all happens repeatedly in the ninth grade corridor
and we are just come back from monuments of Teotihuacan
necking with girlfriends on Lee Ann Meyer's porch
trading ingots of turquoise and silver for the necklaces
to be worn around the ankles in the famous round dance
reconsidered at midnight in the State Hospital edge of town
mushrooms growing in reddish circles being devoured
by maenads who have deserted their husbands for true Love
this is the discourse of Pure Reason the Rights of Man
and the girl with pool dark eyes who speaks flamenco Spanish
in our dreams resonates with the absolute madness
of a musician of the Hermetic transducing collars of Egyptian
into the metamorphic rantings of the purely Dionsyian
because we have been there before and seen by day the Stars
being drunk obsessed infatuated in love dying to die
you bit my nose because I could not wake from intoxication
and there was vomit all over the maps and crystals shattered
it was Beethoven walking on the moon with his brickbat
or Michelangelo thundering out sonnets of angry smoke
in the Vatican of the Underground stained grottos & catacombs
ghosted by the Flea whose immense tragedy mocks ink
it has ever been thus the drugstore with its suspended clock
four-faced beneath which brahmins and mendicants gather
unsure that night will ever come and Rosy dawn again
+++
portents migrations of reddening constellations the Brain!
in a back room with indecision planning for the next One
worlds both miniscule and too immense to measure
flares of Bengal nights and women of impossible nomenclature
wearing designs of heavens in the tangled masses of their hair

bright red the first one to step forth from the orchestra
froth on her bitten lips bracelets serpentine and luxurious
carpets wall hangings waters channeled through rooms
where gopis gather garlands to award the Groom
it is prehistoric the Noise and ceremony of countless gods
small swarming deities creating separate numbers for themselves
blinding profusion of color incense smoking the dusk
azure the perfect hue of what comes from behind hidden
dark matter reading braille the onslaught Robespierre
obscure passages deserted fanes in the middle of nowhere
for no one and transgressions in powder and silk
languid hours of an afternoon becoming godlike
crescent moons gilded like the horns of the Cow
being led through the parade ground for sacrifice
appearing in the evening of the grand ball far far away
exchange of spit kisses tooth to tooth guessing it is Shiva!
countless the eons of orgasm and dysfunction in the tannery
who is who in the Medina when the portico shuts
and the muezzin ascending the stairwell suddenly forgets
these are the hours that should not be counted the ennui
and tedium of lovemaking confused limbs and fever
licking the remains of sex in the Etruscan mirror
who said there's no life like this one? abomination
how far the rills the banks the ridges and haughty cliffs
of planet earth how distantly beautiful to gaze a mist
the fogs and tremblings shouldn't we never do this
again and again the lacquered insouciance dallying
in the next eternity as if it were the present one
shifts in space amassing cloud nebulae for the show
tonight as on no other and fondling the precious things
and revealing a cool smooth thigh and embracing
one after another the desert princesses their mouths
like opened pomegranates dripping the immortal
how so much like the end of time this eventuality
sitting in the basement a nameless girl on the knee
vomiting over page after page of her magazine
glossy photos of a life spent in ambition's boudoir
narcissus and nemesis both shadowy looming

from doom to dust patiently awaiting the Moment
+++
dark matter darker still the
we have come around to the stopping point
going crazy writing this poem as promised
a vision from the memorabilia of Saint Adolf II
enumerating the endless series of cities built one
upon the other in a fuming clepsydra of sky
knowing full well the finish is not an accomplishment
but the tideswell of waves furiously intent on erasing
everything we have over thought or inscribed
undertow of nausea and expectation
blanched subterfuges in a backward script
unable to be deciphered swept away
not knowing whether that is you or I on the other shore
waving something diminished in the small air
what I tried to tell you but missed the opportunity
lingering among the bark and futhark runes
attempting to read in the monoliths of ether
the past of the future in the ninth grade
always night oncoming with its silent chariot
its impressive horses of immaculate dust
its ceaseless redundancies of dark matter
swirling in terrific conflagrations
the dreams within the only dream
little by little the (
a leaf
torn
a voice)

IX

SCHEHERAZADE

spellbound the tale told twice as many times as ever
carpets unfolding magma celluloid editions in heaven

obfuscations penetrations machinations all a story
to weave and to be rewoven on memory's dark loom

the unspeakable to fend off the night mute histories
galactic tapestries spinning enormous silences of time

without beginning or end summation of misspent alphabets
everywhere the tale is the same and of a great disorder

then why I am here why this deathly undressing of skin
the participles of void and renewal cancelled and Loud

relics of cuneiform memorization like sands scattered dry
over the what used to be and never was a city out of time

days sojourned in imagined fields palaces of corrupt stone
lime beds soldered planets linked to a fevered poet's mind

such joinings syllable and syntax words running backwards
to retell the dreaming sleeper's once upon a jot and tittle

forwards prelude the oncoming august storms and thread
a noose through the privy space where thinking's narrow

and spread sheets cool of mint and fresco on the month
when everything is supposed to start again rains and grass

swarms of gods divided among themselves the chirring insect
horde bright sounding the multiple versions of the instamatic

how it was and when the clouds gathered and which was the rock
and which the stone standing on the which god was first to yell

springing forth from the imaginary brow the multiplied species
us the human form and wandering in desert and labyrinth to find

nothing rings the distance to possess and when it was the woman
in me the suspended amulet the breasts to bare the chiding spite

brought by the hair to the citadel a promise sworn to keep and
princess alert to phone and form a voice a clarion in the dawn

opaque succession of chapters warring knife and buckler the shield
the hasp the sudden entry of navigable things athwart the seething stream

will you come home then will you not recognize the in me what was
and yours is only a simple chill a bed beside the unknown lane a bier

here lay the weary thing and rise no more while I this tell you spray
tolling brassy the invisible heights how you fell why you cried where

oceans among us yes and the great crescent moon my Eyes foretell and
asteroids of predication the syllabary of miscomprehension the herself

implicit codes silent vowels the Goddess redefined and enters all shining
white is nothing compared to her shadow the witness of all origins the tongue

to spell and tell and narrate yes the rising waters the broken bridges fords
places where none dare to tread the blind well beside the fallen consonants

and what's more when He came into the quarter and raised his menacing quote
shivering in the dusk a stable horses restless the incontinent and mysterious

how each gave the other warning looks a note in crypto script mirrors
with no backside and wasn't there a great crying and hair pulling and spit

and if you ask me I won't scribble a menace nor pen feathered notes a musk
a music a treble chord everything in the air intangible a scrutiny to moon

fixing where possible the fluid thought a sensation that I am going to faint
placing metered feet in the margins a whistle a thing caught in the throat

to pronounce anything correctly I choke just recalling how angry it was
echo to know exactly what it was the first time all hot and the apron undone

my god what legs what a spindle of a story to rewind how the labored hour
spent its total minutes and the chasm and the abyss and the arroyo blanched

the first star of day the last star of night I wing them in prosaic portraits
careful to shift the meaning in each so as not to resemble too much the Other

then the orders of red like vermilion cinnamon carmine or hues of orange
limes are good to suck and divine the thrust was first meant to tongue mmm

so when he starts talking all notches and wedges the ideolect is so strange
powders and perfume can you see me looking like that all you know ***yellow***

rumors of tribes coming down from the hills spears and boomerangs
shouting animals in human hides using forked sticks to make the earth mean

something else you should be aware the henna on the soles of my feet
the organ grinder whose monkey eats weeks he painted them he loved them

Lotus-Feet he called me and swimming in his eyes I learned to write the Bible
why they call me every so often to revive water-of-life the primary rose the

deluge of course the never ending so don't get too close when I'm doing this
when I'm sewing my fingers to the grass and listen loud to the shut door

lateral supports keep me sleeping while the color blank my favorite floods
the lattice and vine and ichor begins to ooze from the pores of my divinity

another thing this is a stretch of the limit a drawer within a drawer untelling
yakkity yak sleepy boredom the countless anecdotes about sperm and time

until zzz his head falls ho ho heavy and lids of steel tighten sleep's screws
around the tiny disorder of hieroglyphs he has for a brain the filthy sod

why wouldn't you open another bottle why not the next cigarette a smoke
fools them every time winsome standing knee high to the corner in a mini

arabesques sweet mutilations of sound cooing in the reverend ears a shhh
tossing and turning to the radio he cannot hear to the magnificat the slide

I won't go into it anymore not so deep as that the well springs the files
colors iridescent sublime not ashamed to admit I knew them all the brash

so I'm in this predicament this wrap around story hour nodding off the
brown widow's weeds the vulgate the acrimony and ammonia the sandy

parched terrain the mirages the oil digs sheiks in pantomime sheets
shrieking silently you know the balloons of speech that just evaporate

and loves to hear over and over the one about Agamemnon how he got it
turkish baths and the gold crown rolling into pools of pure absinthe

or about Helen and the sphinx near the cataracts of the Nile and the dream
basilisks spitting fire in the burning strand she was no one's anymore

the enigma the variations of the mystery the oracle in the bottle the flies
everything spinning in my head festering scabs on one's knees begging for

I'm his little alpha biddle his remixed concrete his store-front wife
I'm the wharf he leaps from the wig in his ear the constant harp of all

when I think of it and that's always and the renaissance Eye-talians
come up to my memoirs all patent leather and stiletto and hair curly cue

then emboldened my tale to tell swells wide a big sweeping operatic
and the air I fling aside is the passacaglia and chaconne of pure insanity

all panting in my lap and sleep walking his embroidered imaginings
me the quim and pestle of his gawking day mares all a sweat and leather

no wonder it comes back for more the god in the amber glass commands
eventide to roll back its fuss and marchers in the snow pack the windows

what breath that is and halos of sunset lordly passages in the fairy woods
messages scrawled on bark kisses and hugs from Zeus the greek paramour

how many times I do it all and rhyme schemes and puppetry engines knock
about baby's dead in the pudding the queen's in a fitful ire dark is Here

so it rolls night after rocking night reading heightened literary ornaments
from the lies of Herodotus to the Prema-Sagara under the stellar awning

shape of ink sable bordered paragraphs utterances from the vedas huge
compound word formations jungle clusters of inimitable clicks and tweets

who's up there in my tree whose monkey is climbing up my stairs whose
himalayan ex machina jibbering hobson jobson is that discourse anyway

put the 'postrophe in the parenthesis roll your R's jack the knife
I'm all spine for you Sweetums I'm a shiver in the dusk a panting slur

It's all I can do to stop spitting wrapping the snake around my thing
going whumpa whumpa whenever Betelgeuse falls into sight what a mar

suchness of other times I recount breathing in sweetly oleander jasmine
petals fragrant exhumed pinkly shameless unaging whoever I seem to be

girlfriend busty hoyden wench of shahs lusting rutting prinking spanking
all tolled the night's never over reel tides circle round again the wash and flow

ginger plant taj mahal cool for the templed brow mirrored worlds a whirl
gigging jazz fueled into latest hours can I even the score betting journalese

hagiographies lender lease laws of the saints in question the fundament
the loam and truss of planet earth the burning squills the parched and hell

shall I never this night end this hour rolling back the stone to find the pit
and shouting's all around the chamber sword and taint flux sweating words

chanting chanting the invented sigh give the once over to raja what's his name
the blue finned devil champing at the bit all bone and saw buzzing through

chastened never and folds the map up and silver lake's small oval size
pour molten gold down's throat and quick write the prescription

all's a dying in the bosom my hasp has no quick the quivering aimlessness
these plots only thicken and search lights my eyes scour the burdened lore

how will it end this tale of Maya's *come on Baby let the good time's roll*
is it all about me little alpha bit switching the Muse's twitch the demon

hindsight gives me no qualms I'd nivver again do it like forefront first
giving him the chub of my fist and driving the quill deep into the trauma

penning one mendacity after another drilling it up all frothy and bejeweled
words you know that come from nowhere universes of inky night the Stars!

rehearsing the devil's funeral endgame of chess hunters mocking Old Tyger
drinking of the witcup and rounding rills on the moon's argent instrument

how they take it and drub it to death wanting all the same a fame old tyme
virtue's disregard disrobing pleat by pleat the simple frock I seem to wear

were it not for the skin of the song I've outdone Frozen in the back seat
motor still running below zero's to know what I drink talking outta my head

and there's so much more I wanna tell you so much more I wanna say
but look Dawn's put on her rub and it's time for me to smoke my helium

yes and it's sad we're all in this yarn driveling spools around the teaser
and me jawing and jamming away scat singing who's listening to this

nonsense voodoo argot pidgin talk anyway how many were the victims
and why were they nameless the difference between a just and unjust act

resonates like glass on the distant hill a seesaw light hemming its way
or I am lost spook talking this nightly shanty where hovel bare I lay

waiting for the exegesis this has been a royal rant I've had my toss
the mighty had their flay the small in their ecumene of dust and lice

a sort for want of crime I'd love to spoor a little more but echo's fade
my joe's gone ashes my memory's bitter silt this woe for all is done

FIAT LUX!

X

BHAKTI

I will now sing of those
whose minds are turned to wanton bees
of kings tossed like chameleons into blind wells
of those for whom chastity is nothing
who fling themselves unclad into Desire's embrace
of girlfriends who have abandoned their senses
running amok in groves of pestilence and ire
to reach through altered worlds the Lotus Feet
sing I now the mad frenzied dance of those
who can no longer comb their tousled hair
letting slip gown and bodice to their feet
drum pounding cymbal slashing dark ether
sweat beaded faces lost all control eyes rolled back
of brahmans quarreling over cattle
lost to the dharma to be reborn hundredfold
reddened by ego-fires chattering nonsense
until drowned repeatedly in the Ocean of Being
they resurface remembering the only One
smoking Bang like never before turning green
of the ones who become adulteresses for a touch
the nipple in the palm a smoldering turned and spun
nostrils fuming for the divine spirit invisible
the Unformed god the tool chiseler the deviant mocker
sing then of the ones sculpted from air full blown
wearing brass pendants the weight of mountains
in the earlobes and bangles up and down the arms
leaping shamelessly in robes of yellow dust
or hiding in mango groves ripe as the fruit itself
breasts hanging as if from branches to be plucked
in love with an idol a statue a print a painting
discovered in a book coloring the courtyard hues of red
iridescent spirals whorls of cinnamon and pepper
incense so thick the soul drowns wavering across
ready to plunge into the seething roils of

and sing I too the betrayed the paramours in white
inscribing things memorized in dreams
on curling palm-leaf loud humming deaf as ants
parading insanely up and down bamboo stalks
looking for the honey pot the dipper the ladle
mouths wide open moist wet dripping with
juice of the forbidden fruit the sticky denseness
kissing being kissed unarmed barefaced
sluts shaking their hips in the noontime blaze
when nothing can be seen and nothing
exists to see mirage in shimmering sheets of light
a whirl of voices of snatches of song like skin
tattered ripped from the bone dangling in memory
of those transduced from the original tongue
written and rewritten in the dialects of hill and swamp
verdant lush passages of the immarginable
descriptions transferred from tobacco plant to ivy
coinciding with the theosophist's amalgam
mercury and gold fluted columns of night-air
something that has never been tranced and
I sing now of those whose passion is betrayal
fundamentally skewed in favor of the dead
who live intransigent as seers in the second sleep
who rising from beds of live coals Breathe
and the ones who are sideways come first and
the upside down and the backwards and the
ululating in pitch high voices the love Supreme
carving inches of sperm in the sand writhing
spinning darkening even as dawn threatens its ray
motioning to one another quietly assaulting
the ones who are deaf to reason who demand
always to be in the front of the abracadabra
the unreal omegas the who and the who are not
being as one in plasma and cosmetics
adorned superabundant in jewelry dazzling
because they are incoherent stumbling
vomiting on the divan where the god-form lay
sing I then who on the roof display their meat

to the sun and pray in a pidgin Sanskrit in whiteness
to the blank and ovoid to those who open
wantonly their legs to the cloud-gods whose rain
descends in a torrent of black sulfur
to impregnate the witless virgins who piss
ecstatically on the temple floor like dogs
and are cursed and reviled and are sent shunned
out the back door for having had commerce
with the Unseen and who employ osiers on their backs
parading pig-faced in the alley ways
summoning from their dormers the Citizens
How much is this madness a pure joy!
torn a hank of hair in the hand the finger excised
in the soft grass the lips bruised overmuch
no one knows the self the other is lost in time
much of what I sing is the longing gone
the tremendous aching to recall exactly what
but a dew drop a pebble shining alone
on the path which was once the Way
where errant ghosts thin as reeds stray
wearing raiment the color of sand oblivious
of the pyramid that entombed them once
always searching even after 84,000 deaths
the suchness of the thrill the opaque
the Dance in the stifling ballroom summer hour
hands aloft heads bobbing senselessly
memory a thing of the past nothing solid but
the intangible glove that fits over the soul
and the music drum shell bamboo reed tin can
clappers tomtom the variegated turmoil
cacophonous loud super rhythms outside the body
voudoun mojo mohenjo daro dollar shill
and the ones who are silver coruscating in the sky
who are shooting stars feet lifted off earth
moving and not moving to the silent commands
that impel us out of the nerve gut into
the immense boundlessness of frozen space

haunted by the name the soft lesions shading off
into syllables barely pronounced the vedic chant
hair locks strewn over pearl beaded brows a sweat
sheets body indivisible from body the levers that
lift to heaven and the great suspended lakes eerie
moonlit surfaces shaking the wimpled wave sheen
illumined inwards the cast whispering divine shift
reds across milky shaking breasts wet and heavy
darkness the name soft skins haunted night scene
shades plied through tresses unkempt barely off
strewn matted against cheeks the fevered blush
like syllables without echo the stressed vowel a
sweet indivisible from body other than lifted by
levers into a heaven of suspended lakes a sheen
reflecting lunar faces wimpled quivering waters
of shaft shivering strewn pearls illumined wave
shifts reddening indivisibly between body's weight
shading shifting shapes of the name brows wet
and fruit as heavy idioms hill and swamp eerie
voices vedic chant lifted off earth inches from
chains of indivisible nature watering swift a
beds arisen from abandoning husbands spittle
connected tongue to red fevered hush the cheek
scattered locks matted night sweat the syllables
did I pronounce the berlitz manual lunar stress
echo vowels designed to rotate reflecting moon
sounds sandy mounts shoreline decibels later the
haunting name occluded clusters retroflex clicks
consonants black in nature drop beside the well
kings turned to chameleons pitched blindly inner
dancing illuminations ghostly against the wall
diachronic voices jungle dialect voudoun swell
breasts like darkening fruit wet eerie touching
milky space broadening dream woof the loam
warm earth spices incense dense dusky smokes
echo bluish spell cheeks blushed the hush a wave
illumined rotting underfoot the mulch of time
dancing inches from planet earth hands aloft

arms stiffened in trance the indivisible body of
hill and swamp a drop beside the blind well kings
turned to chameleons tossed into syllables pitched
sounds shady clusters mango groves soft as breasts
heaving fevered in the flush manual rotating bliss
dense dusky incense sandalwood cinnamon peppers
bright touching excised fingers forbidden the name
a husk softening shadows a lesion a skin a voice
bleeding in the leaf torn and chewed the baleful
in a trance I'm in a

the mystical union with the Other when I was in love
with obsessed with totally out of my mind for echo vowels
of her the goddess transmuted was I sick and who in
her celluloid transductions skin softened beyond blond
alliteration it was devotion beyond the senses to what
and seek in books how the why is which suchness of
blindly tossed into the well like a king-transformed
chameleon dark hooded night was upon me and sound
by sound uttered the name lisping slightly bruised lips
imagined until one was the Other me was no more
a sylph apparition half clad shimmering before the lens
I could be *her*! I could be *her*! drowned in the sea of Being
raveled in silk slips torn lingerie nylon stockings spit
going under with bad lipstick and processed hair all
peroxide and dumb too smoking helium cheroots prinked
out dazzled and daffy on a non-existent sidewalk loony
sweating it out with liters of vile red wine while Bong!
the television reproduces a noon in hell teen angel
gang bang in triplicate screen goes dubba dubba
and there is she Mystical you said it Union herself
the other me of myself dashed in browns and ground
to a cinnabar pulp talking all outta my Brazilian head
each is every for the other you all know that

it's this rotating device in the middle
you can't separate it from the head wind
in the book version twins are born to the soul mother

and unable to cope she sets them circling
around the sun whirring faster and faster
and down below these mechanical beings
these entities born and reborn without a why
to their name dumbfounded all a staring into the ether
azure blue horizon of circling visions look!
night and day body and soul all in One
transmogrified sent chittering into the trees
pretend to live while really dying
inventing one after another small gods to interpret
it's love quite simply that sets them going
making big houses burning incense
drawing pictures using their imagination
it's mother in the end large soft Beautiful
spawning in mysterious waters
going away and coming back every summer
a doll in each hand a way of talking
you just wanna die for Her

XI

NEKUIA

"ai! com s'en van tuit mei amic"
Cercamon

alpha

drinking malt liquor out of brown paper bags
we sat there in the june sun not knowing
what to say to one another conscious only
of the dark dimension that had spread over
like an inexplicable legend the park rotting
green fetid asphalt garbage spilled city summer
throw wine sops to the three headed dog
or maybe the words were there we just hadn't
found them being philosophically silent
ragged edges of time the stifling air sirens

that create a distance between now and forever
or it is somewhere else hills sick with winter
perhaps waiting for the meadowlark's song
still the two of us not sure of the context
had there been a quarrel a difference of
never mind the peaceful before us spread
its map across imagined arcadian fields
the bounty of thoughts the Ionian spring
utter delusion of being human and
still drinking booze out of brown paper bags
would ever return this moment's interstices
memorial greens budding behind the pages
whiter than longing the next minute of time
throw wine sops to the three headed dog
the two of us separated by the unfathomable
yet the whatness the sheer over the beyond
couldn't get over the mystery of the illness
the sudden randomness of convulsions spit
visiting in the steep unconscious the gods
who illumine and just as baffling take away
the world turning around on its skewer
a double amputee named Hera remembering
her brazen white arms her supple shoulders
standing at stair top weapon in hand dreams
it is still somewhere else and we're at a wake
or after the funeral a brilliant sun in our dark
suits for mourning the brown paper bag passing
between us in a somber sort of mythology trees
talking at us leaning against a wind hazy blown
faces emerge to recognize rising from earth shafts
in fist fully risen warriors sleeping their tumble
the bad liquor in our mouths we laugh choking
before the illumination hits the big spark red
throw wine sops to the three headed dog
explosive arguing about what came first songs
or the small birds in their chaucerian latin or
imagining the provençal landscape of Vincent Van Gogh
thick yellow slashes of afternoon so blinding

like a deity converted to pure light buzzing almost
electricity in the rampant bushes whose funeral
the name is now just a label in cold alabaster
like the time windows became a mysterious cloud
and the figures behind them sticking tongues out
immense and horrible why we didn't suspect
because the full term of the intoxication hiss
couldn't you tell by the way my head fell to
and you kept on talking about Gide and Camus
and why years later on some sordid park bench
silently understanding ourselves without a vowel
gilded excrescent moments ripped out of time
dehiscent envelopes of grass or hair to recall
a sunday fishing with gramps on a lakeside
in Ojibway country placid fusion of air and indigo
caught two or three sunfish watching them flop
gasping for life then stone dead wet glistening
throw wine sops to the three headed dog
isn't the illness like that which descended so rapidly
riding fast in the car the horn honking all the
way to Brooklyn Jewish Hospital the fever
unabated millions of nights crystallized in
a single moment when consciousness flees
forever altered you thought it was like death
and it should be so wet glistening on the back
seat of the car honking the horn all the way
from the lake back to the kitchen where
granny would pan fry them for supper before
listening to radio programs like Fred Allen
the evening brown redolent of old tobacco
in his leather rocker gramps dozing in german
or the dandelions he made us pick in the heat
of the most interminable noon ever forcing
bunches of plucked yellow heads in brown
paper bags like the ones we were drinking
from in that ragged unkempt park in 1978
and putting his foot down to crush them
to make way for even more dead yellow heads

the way we felt too after the funeral wilting
the warm liquor in our empty stomachs to
burn even more intensely the illumination
we wanted to feel looking at a horizon empty
of everything but the resilient metal water tower
as if it would collapse in a second before us
like a dream the terraced green slope embarked
to a street so distant it could no more be real
the metropolis of asphalt and rubber spinning
which was your city which was mine in the atlas
throw wine sops to the three headed dog
the funeral the way the face looked waxen for
eternity on its silken cushion don't look twice
lying there wet and glistening on the back seat
all the way to Brooklyn Jewish the traffic as if
underwater in slow motion hand on the horn
and full grown the warriors in Grecian armor
with spears in their fists tossed clods at one
another starting a quarrel internecine strife
forming leagues of tiny city states and islands
when a man could walk a kingdom in a day
the sun burning down its clepsydra half gone
how does one return from the house of the dead

"Glorios Dieus, a vos me clam,
car mi toletz aqels qu'ieu am"

beta

and went down one by one into the unlit chamber
a basement reeking of human urine and winter coal
shades among shades we were become not knowing
nor touching not feeling what it was knocking against
bodies without shape as if lifted from trodden earth
someone crying behind the spent furnace thin reedy
whining rust on the tongue dried spit the unshaved jaw
who could know teeth gnashing dreaming gnarled
branches leaves torn for the nature of their voices
appeal to the sibyl a sudden wind stale and dusty

words blown into full size the oracle of faded ink
mingling souls stunned and dazed looking for shapes
which once belonged to them in ruined tenements
of skin and cancer eaten bone residue of
here stood who once shone prideful mighty Ajax
a stirring of lice in the ragged mattress devastated
the seer's eloquence trails off into a wet blur
of indistinct consonants a mirage of phonetic decay
weather stripped vehicles junked and toppled
into the rising mud and hands the remnants of
knuckle thumbs twisted back reach out to us
do we know anyone any more is there a common bond
what were once men our comrades brothers allies
it isn't very far from here is it the exit I mean
the depth charges that implode the soul's empyrean
fugue of a million petty galaxies behind the eyelid
the place behind the pile of rags a little warmth
scratching in the ear an echo some splinter of sound
was it a song way out in the sandy reaches of nowhere
could hear the single string plucked and some words
found them on the floating island south of Delos
now just masses of incoherence heard on an old radio
listen to the night where it once was star streaked
comes back to us in snatches of light so archaic
it cannot mean a meandering here shuffling in dirt
memory is a flower whitened behind glass
alone pale evanescent not the glorious morning
when was that who were the ones walking with us
what highway was it northbound and the carriers
the ants in hordes blindly scurrying to find their god
beside a dried lake bed where as children the heroes
tossed dice in a game that lacks orientation houses
moved as if by chance from one tropic to another
floating gardens smoking volcanoes in the bluish far
one was named Pepito the others who were they
walking with us of a morning yellow with light
cicadas on either side of the road in dense fields
chirring endlessly before the call to arms to growth

full blown men with shadows hurrying into distance
here now knocking weightless forms like rice bags
sodden dirty the unbidden dark our wanderings
to no end in black maze five fathoms below
what do names matter applied to these inert heaps
this was one once Achilles beloved of Apollo!
and of Helen the moon-faced what remains
a forked smear in shifting rubble inky miasma
what can ever take us back to the hull to the tall masts
to the waves that bear light from the depths
roseate apparitions in constantly changing liquid
for there is nothing firm nothing that brings back
memory of ivy and fiercely coruscating Mind

gamma

laying on the traced ground these
          steaming plates *the city of Dis*
                with trembling and unutterably
where a few pebbles   strewn
    tracks of ox-carts leveled by rain
did you remember to bring
             not sure where the entrance is
the place with a sprig of parsley
how fresh it was here the april
             barley cakes small and white
this was the fallen blanket
        this was the waxing and the waning
   at the gate stoned the doormen stare
guessing who can and who can no longer be
     among the numbered missing a blank
storms raging within the inch
  summer when both of us lying there
a brown paper bag passing back and
  talking about Camus and Gide
delusion of being human
         the large hand coming from the cloud
and the straps around the head
      and the thunder grievous loud

whose funeral it was and the music stray
gravel underfoot the immense
a voice that hardly from somewhere deep
mind like a tomb ants flowing east and west
the time angel hit the ground 100 mph
nowhere left to go and strewn brains
seeds lying there blackened a
heat in its metal cylinders circling
the star that governs all
from top to bottom at least
one thousand million light years
and still waiting on the hillside one early
listening to the troubadour song
Guillaume IX of Poitiers **riding**
unsaddled his piebald horse and
the two girls what were their names
fatally attractive one blond the other
like a raven her jet hair glistening
in a trance lips protruding down
below sound of traffic buzz and hum
near the famous greek restaurant
whose back room smoke filled
and the murmurings and ravings
of fully grown warriors bent over
green baize pool tables
is the entrance to Hades
one has to put however unsure
a hand on the brass knob turn twice
counter clockwise and slowly descend
hear the muffled moan like beasts
blinded cattle on a gang plank
in their midst Ulysses his ear holes
pierced by the shrill sea waves
turned to glass deathly calm
noon when the ladies disrobe
becoming as liquid silk
their firm buttocks rippling
bellies slightly convex snouts

like pigs blazing nostrils
bluish haze in their eyes
corn flowers dogwood jasmine
never see again
sky like pumice a yearning
a cigarette endlessly flaring
here place small sesame buns
and recall achingly the voice
before it disappeared into a hole
beside the cut grass pour a libation
dark red the fuming wine
sacred to Bacchus who never
did us good

delta

come to terms with the teenage bodhisattva
whose alcoholic death
was only an echo of the earlier illness
the bout with consciousness the warnings
from far off sri lanka about *attachment*
everything is an imitation
quotations from an ineffable past
maelstroms of consciousness swirling
small white buds like planets astray
can mean nothing under the bridge
below by the rushing underground water
where the grim boatman waits
his will be sweet wafers russian cakes
semolina and honey sprinkled

throw wine sops to the three headed dog

XII

ΚΑΣΣΑΝΔΡΑ

standing on the high school steps raving
Apollo spat in her mouth and cursed her he did
isn't red the angry color and which team will win
arms raised voice grown hoarse barking signals
aren't the stars to come out by four this afternoon
isn't the ball to be passed secretly to the Russians
the violin in her head with its endless chaconne
insists on the destruction of cosmic order
divinations at the soda fountain about sex with whom
she allies herself with the shadows that climb walls
of their own accord painting yellow the heights
listens intently to the radio in her brain
messages messages from the various chthonic deities
mud splattered bleary eyed filthy from ruination
who code her mutilated and passionate embraces
no one listens
iterations of the divine spark in lunar berlitz
from the chasms of her lips fables of the bees
detonations of silent clouds in the gymnasium
where the fellows tease her madly tearing her clothes
"come on, Cassie, give us a kiss" permutations
of the most archaic verb known to man *Fuck*
shouldn't she get it right just once?
stands there on the steps at rush hour in mantic dash
of syllables and sputtering the big rant about the Horse
the noon hour climax the hashed vortex behind the shed
giving head to Poseidon of the billowing waves
"you're *basura*, Cassie" a wetback whispers biting her ear
she's a hex she's a witch she's the devil in disguise
when asked "is there life after high school?"
the harlequin in her stolen sequins and embroidery pouted
suspecting full well the dark price of prescience
mind-body formula breaks down in her utterances
Apollo's spit turns to ashes on her voluble tongue

sees amazing conflagrations shipwrecks mosquito wars
aggravated vision of symbiotic treachery
eyeballs of the gods perforated by sulfuric myths
jilted at the prom a bouquet of bleeding rosebuds
broken promises string of scatological insults
because she wouldn't go down for Apollo
what's a girl to do but go nuts stark raving nuts
it's all in greek the topsy turvy tale of a woe
gone wrong and her dizzy from the noon time reefer
wearing a white top knot in her hair all oracle
buzzing in the insectary of her madness spouts
grief after grief in a tragedy of baths and knives
foreboding illicit births the twins she would never see
yet intransigent on the concrete steps stands there shaking
with the godhead somewhere inside her shouting
"don't go there tonight! it's all gonna burn!"
no one listens
wearing bobby socks and penny loafers a plaid skirt
with a big brass safety pin and a cashmere sweater
bobbing her head up and down to a secret rhythm
the tom-tom drum the triangle and the maze
she knows who the ghouls are in their insect trysts
Troilus and Criseida Palamon Arcite and Emilye
it's back and forth up and down the stairs
crisp autumn wind in her hair a narcotic fix in her gaze
who wants to date her who wants to get anywhere near
frothing at the mouth marring the big red lipstick
starts talking latin from out of nowhere
"declarat viridique advelat tempora lauro"
chewing the bitter bay leaf absolutely delphic
nostrils flaring a bluish vapor she exhales strongly
stomps her foot breaks out in beads of pearly sweat
talks the talk of death in strict dactylic hexameter
"effusaeque genis lacrimae et vox excidit ore"
such is the strength of her voice the peremptory insanity
that none dare approach not even her brother Paris
contempt abject hysteric syllogisms exhorted a mile a minute
who will drive her car tonight who will light the bonfire

will the home town team really lose as she hallucinates
will the captain be dragged around the stadium a hundred times
headless and bewildered at the sudden visit to Hades
will the goons from the enemy squad rush taking her captive
it's just a couple of blocks walk to the public library
where in swoon over a volume called The Loom of Language
she convulses in a fit of sexual delirium
being transported in a haze to a paleolithic Anatolia

Apollo god of light and music spat in her mouth
and cursed her stripping her mind of its white raiment
she can be anywhere she can be in the future of eternity
she can be strolling down second street humming madly
the song from Moulin Rouge "where is your heart?"
she can be a love slave Agamemnon's own little sweetums
or she can be dreadful matted locks red-eyed fuming
at the top of the stairs adolescent breasts exposed grimy
anklets of filth byzantine pendants five stone each in her ears
the marble lions at the gate reduced to rubble by her look
darting venom and hatred like a desert basilisk
liquid shadow of her twin Helenus prophesying galactic collapse
or she can be girlfriend fork-tongued duplicitous cute
dimple cheeked wavering between athletes for the dance
non-committal unreasonable tease with her bouffant hair
and adult stiletto heels parading in her underwear
before the photograph of her favorite warrior Diomedes
ceaselessly casting aspersions on the future of the war
knowing how darkness will take her by the waist doubling her
in a powder of storms where raped and defiled she will exult
riding a swift Achaean skiff back to Mycenae
to the sleeping fortress with its maze of corridors and stairwells
night in every corner and the silent roaring of the dream
in which Klytemnestra wearing elevator shoes and a french wig
waits for time's intricate hair trigger to go off

I am the size of ink a spelling traced across incendiary
skies lost this rant obfuscations in the key of delta minor
sketching improbable omegas the end of time's round dance

pulsing quasar in the left hemisphere where disorganization
takes place the dismounting of the moon crater by crater
whiteness of the abject the misplaced the unwanted I am
circling stairs that go nowhere ascending into the mind's rump
a travesty of woman obliged to spend my skin on the empty
cosmetics of sand the defiles and wastelands my domain
at last the bottomless well smoke incense and black fumes
sulfuric language that pours out of me unwilling as I descend
the precarious temporal ladder into the tannery to color
what I see the various sessions of red that are distilled
from the hides of mythical beasts and implore the gods
the five thousand eight hundred of them who torment me
to give me sense to take from my madly prattling tongue
the bristling vocabulary of the etruscan nightmare script
left steaming on the mirrors of Hades and I am this raving
darkened vowels spitting against the wrists of my captors
inverted curses of the god of light and music hallucinations
this intuition of heights and verticality of mental excesses
bordering on the purely insane putting nothing up for sale
other than my own mind stripped of its white raiment
saliva and bile and sour milk and sperm lathered face
that goes on and off like a traffic signal bright red crimson
parting the seas that erupt from the innermost psyche
and green and slowly yellow and dying beside the potter
whose poetry revolves endlessly on his humble wheel
is I am the ink a size more than I can measure a poem
too could be the insane most part of the psyche I am a rant
omegas tumbled out of the cave and set me up on the top
why does no one listen to ink the ineffable the darkness
where the stairs can go no further up and beyond to circling
seven spheres each the less than the other in suchness of
perfection I am the gloss and the logos desperately abuzz
for the introspection of silence the muse unbeckoned me a
section of water the outer remove of ice the fiction of smoke
odorless skin a song too bitter to recall a light yes a light
that too falling apart on the stairs with me only me
a small portion of space defined by the contours of sand
a thought that I am predicting to be a season of fire and

slowly brought around to beds of consciousness adrift a
folly the slave of love to some purulent dirty old king his ink
his defiled little smut of a thing when I was a princess once
a wavering robed one with a staff and spoke to snakes
in the dark and learned from them secrets of ink and spelling
to rave against the oncoming and to see and seeing know
it is come to smallness a notch in the air a something that
cannot be defined other than by the running noise it makes
sleeping easier now beside the fallen lions whose stone talking
like a drunk in the oven considers the variations of ink the spill
so many words of the many none that make sense

the part where the poem opens up and
the dusty path zigzagging from the ruins of Troy
when I remember her in her fluted robes wind caught
hair tangled by the air's mutinous voices
the poem endangered by its own direction
barefoot on the steep stone steps below heaven
how could it be she that I would fall in love with
moving writing tools and ink wells and parchment
when the poem stops to make a light shine
she did not look my way never not once
enmeshed in her incantations and ravings
as if conducting a chorus of invisible maenads
me a few steps below looking up in adoration
spit fire glosses of the forbidden and reviled
ten cities built one upon the other absolute rubble now
and I am dreaming about her feet her hips shaking
how old can she be for me the unbidden poet
she can be twelve or fifteen but not eighteen!
mantic oracular crimson mouth moving wordlessly
though worlds of ink that obliterate all poetry
the edifices in her eyes green jasper emerald hell towers
threatening to collapse at any minute to dust
to years of moiling roiling dust universes
or it is the eye-blackening that stains her cheeks
and I am on a grey quadruped going uphill
the afternoon has lost its gongs all is fade and dun

tinsel hangs in the air a muezzin falls asleep
in the middle of the Call so much heat is in the ether
muffled by blankets of time everything becomes indistinct
yet she is there clear outline of skeleton and moss
on the rant against war and helium dirigibles
she has been to Gallipoli and is destroyed by what she saw
the poem weaves in and out of her skirts
the poem diaphanous against her emblazoned skin
tattoos irreverent love lyrics episodes of dying
from the separation of body and soul
gas structures begin to ricochet against Envy
no one listens to her not even I
making the poem circle her bereft shadow
eating the traces of her footprints in the dusky lime
becoming something other than what it intended
the poem the poem the poem
for ΚΑΣΣΑΝΔΡΑ

XIII

SORTES VIRGILIANAE

(i)

Talia flammato secum dea corde volutans
the goddess turning the cord flaming in her tales
herself spinning the fates under earth the wiles
her heart sectioned willing as darker skies near
will it be capsized the bark adrift roaring among
waves and shoals espy through divine mists a
score to keep in the now empty Olympian halls
where masks hanging on mossy walls leer envy
to make of her robe its pleated agonies turning
her cords tightens the lyre her buskins the crown
tinsel and sage and aromas of meat offerings rise
from some peninsula down below where wearied
her devotees sweat and mud streaked on knees

approaching night in vain appeal suppliant dense
her dusky form to make herself present a bared calf
her firm blanched arms the tunic off the shoulder
turning her volatile weapon first at the flaming
then plucks the cord volumes of sound a tension
dispels and lets fly the shaft from its bed into
high the almost burning air where the first stars
signal the poem's imminence the underfoot twigs
snapping the proximity perhaps of the enemy

(ii)

"Heu fuge, nate dea, teque his" ait "eripe flammis"
hey, born of goddess, yourself and these too take
the rest of your stuff from the flames it's too hot
this morning for this business and be off running
through yon woods a flare can't you see the holy
is on fire the voice as it told you will no longer hear
though you have ears too and scrap the words you
wanted to use as a hostage to the deity of ineffability
rip from the embers what you can of your soul useless
though it be on the journey to the underground house
and Herculaneum is already burnt so you can't go
that way and subterfuges abound the fugue the torn
the snatches from the ashes whose ghostly faces
you conjure fearing as always to tear the flesh
in the wrong place and offer up this dead animal
that was once someone's soul a revisited entity
from some Pythagorean past the parting is cruel
the embers still too hot your fingers scorched again
raving as you do with a filament of music so thin
the air can scarcely bear it and clouds ruddy as kine
threatening noon with a tempest growing fierce
purple as thunder the night-born and then lost

(iii)

et lunam in nimbo nox intempesta tenebat
and moon in limbo held by tempestuous night
what was and was not visible in these dank woods

where confused you revolve in a lunar maze unsure
what it was you said or did losing the divine nimbus
the cloud fret of torrents that swept you from the main
and your comrades your shipmates forever in the drink
drowned caught in Poseidon's azure nets as the oracle
predicted had you not been otherwise and proud stiffly
rejected the news that a goddess was from the moon
descended in the whereabouts of dewy Fiesole of a dawn
you attached little significance to this homecoming and
mourned your late friends their shipwrecked fate
and those far off days clear and bright in sunny Umbria
where shepherd among shepherds in innocence you kept
to the rocks and familiar river banks tuning your pipe
beneath the oak shadow making a poem of the fair Amaryllis whom you have never yet seen but whose
dusky presence accompanies you now in this
deep and intricate wood from which there is no route
unless the goddess repenting shows you her white sign
in the darkening underbrush and you feel keenly desire

(iv)

Quis tibi tum, Dido, cernenti talia sensus
whilom, Dido, discerning you tally your senses
the makeshift love that tore you from the weeds
and now you foment the flames that will make you
senseless to the world a ball of mist wandering afar
taking with it what you most treasured of the heart
in death all things are equidistant, Dido, whisk
from what you feel thoughts of being again and
with whom you surrendered your senses now that
dark and its subhuman total grips you from feet up
and seizes the spine and works its verses into
your still yearning brain, Dido, do not your eyes
discern the revoked trust of earth the fierce ague
of shapes that come to enchant with human delusion
what in fact is infernal the passion to become Other
do you not hear the noon heat like a mountain
of maddened cicadas involving you in a voluptuous

blaze, Dido, and sobbing is of no moment undress
the skin of its white innuendos embarking as you
will on the deathless barge where ash and tears
mingle their ancient tale the one of pain and error
whilst above forever the black sun burns its soul

(v)

certus iter fluctusque atros aquiline secabat
certainly iterated the flux atrocious the cyclone
deeper dark the throes of elimination light despairs
section by section the river gives up its flow
winds that cut deep from the south the simoon
parches life's fertile vale and a desert becomes
where once stood the city glorious the nimbus crowned
thither we once dallied under porticoes of blue shade
listening to the fountain's splash in quarters hidden
from common view our love to share in sweet embrace
shuttered from the sun's immense landscape and
now that memory shimmers like a mirage wafting
in time's mid day ceremony tender fluted breezes
wrapping the soul in its prolonged ecstasy while
the body drops its ivied perceptions one by one
green unfolding from the panoply of divine gifts
shafts of endlessness in hints of dream that
just as soon disappear to make us ask were we
ever there within the camera's inverted eye
certain that the next iteration of breath the flow
that issues from boundless light would us unite
instead of shifting us sundered to this sandy sleep

(vi)

Multa inter sese vario sermone serebant
much intersection with varied sermon seeded
when cleft from the sun's great error wandering
our souls pitiful relics mourn the loss of gravity
the main deflected from the eaten shore to loss
and heavy heads recollect what was once a depth
the varied hues the weight of words the grasses

beneath our shadows inflected as if by a music
too distant to recall and shapes rococo the ginger
slight the tongue's soft romance now darkened
ever in this cage dimensionless of flighted lives
sore much by what had seemed to be above
there in the light by leaf and water running hard
why didn't you ever call back to me why leave me
in this closet dank of never more the stone the pith
cannot the ever steep its misty lore again the while
suchness you over slide and dusky throats silence
in glades of afternoons without memory and
this quiet moment resides interposed you and me
nor quells the sermon with its paragraphs of silence
the interlude we named between our ears conscious life
this braided air that twines breath to another end

(vii)

exim Gorgoneis Allecto infecta venenis
at once Allecto the fury infected with the Gorgon's
poisoned tresses us assails in our passing randomness
nor know to what avail this savage brands our trail
smoking distances canyons of immense the shaded
nowhere to turn the ire inverted to our souls
and swells the sick rankling to the brain infested
how to see now the rim of stars the azure bowl
dipping into eternity's far western hemisphere
leaving us wretched mortals cast on shoals bleak
hopeless introspection the cloud wracked brain's
futile memory of innocence tossed into furious waters
seething the adjectives that toil reddening the pearl
what simmers just below the skin if not anger's
trenchant coil and in the cane-break sifting rage
ash by ash until boils over the third half of earth
and the whole goes into the fray victim of hybris
overweening and we doff our masks and betray
what was human in us delusion and error love's
long straying from the center so why can't you
and find it difficult to allay the three raving Sisters

whose spume and venom pollute the air darkening

(viii)

Reddidit una bovum vocem vastoque sub antro
renders a bellowing voice bull-like within the cave
sub lunar madness to find a way out reconfiguring
the vast geometries of the epic that have led us
so far astray drifting like stunned bees in the stifling
perfume stung wardrobe of Circe rooting like pigs
in great error and devastation can almost hear
sea-waves pounding green depths in the fatal ear
or drum tattoos of legend and memory hoarse
in the irreversible grasses of a mythic childhood
spent in lush reverberation of bamboo & oaten reed
dissonances now I don't want to I'm not the person
I used to be weathering these antiquities of noise
entering caverns and grottos in the search for some
one thing a recollection of or maybe the melody
the registers of tempo beating in the back brain
the dance what is it shadow plays against a cliff
somewhere ever so distant and the tide swells
drawing out the smoke and luster a febrile song
terrible to hear like a wreckage a flotsam a dirge
threnody in black weeds draped revolving crazily
through rock quartz a signal from the beyond of

(ix)

(quot prius aeretae steterant ad litora prora)
quoted first the aerial stuttering a literal prowess
so finally stood and on the shore prior winds
a vague calumny the gods who smite us unawares
on the sandy bluff high to watch the sinking fleet
fired by dreams then fallen felled by invisible fists
can it be we never sailed to Troy nor burnt the hawsers
watching sleepers the ancient thing assail billowed
waves the length of a tormented hour succumbed
is there time enough to photograph the eclipse?
who brought us to this forlorn and wasted zone

spent stars accent the absent mind like brassy prows
stumbled forth from the dead mango grove to light
shun the bees! afternoon the immense buzzing red
nowhere to turn and safeguard the tender vision
adjustable angles foreign paths inward and astray
is there an adjective to describe this lateral tilt?
we faint we vomit we need to learn to sit in chairs
already evening spreads its fogs across the heath
lost beyond counting we forget where the knee
roves where the hand tills where the eye retreats
undone the recollection of grass the dew bestrewn

(x)

vos etiam, Gemini, Rutulis cecidistis in agris
Twins! you've fallen anon into the rutilating fields
you twain in acrid spirits will your selves ever rise again?
but for the circling maze of the seventh heaven you'd
both be sundered forever from the main and to houses
separate return the dazed shadows of a solar error
pick up those bruised photographed others of a childhood
lost in the antipodes far from the asphodel fields
is this trail of white pebbles a sign from the goddess?
easy now sit your weary selves on these folding seats
do look about into the dark hedges start up no more
paper skies painted your favorite blue for a moment
only then to smoke return the vast unknown empyrean
each of you describe this gyre's burning revolution
behold the artist's eye shared by the kaleidoscope
flames a literature of blazing silences the fierce
distinctions of sound and breath until utterly gone
the last traces the futile tracks the white pebbles
Twins! you too rutilating like unseen stars in the far
archaic as the flowers that bear you into summer fields
pomegranate and eglantine the goddess from her hand
scatters black seeds brooding her great blank brow

(xi)

dat gemitum rumpitque has imo pectore voces

gives a groan and breaks from the depths these voices
innuendos of dawn to never be the incessant waves
of darkness the chiding of unfriendly gods the enormous
walkabout in death country catching the chill and agony
why didn't he listen on the day he set forth why didn't he
gives another groan moaning his hapless fate these voices
torn from leaves and into the dusky unknown circles
feet grown old trying and everywhere smell of mulch
underfoot the rank undergrowth sacred to Persephone
perspiring in mortal night sweats not a light in sight
not even a distant flare a city of labyrinthine structure
giving voices from the depths trying to keep breath
in rhythm to the memories of life up above in the blaze
of noon with its intoxicants and girls but some fatal error
what was it the mocking of the myth the stumbling across
the horizon that defines a man's life the imprudent reckless
keeps groaning drawing voices from the deep the multiple
with their rush of words in all directions like the bag of Aeolus
scattering winds of loosed syntax into the vortex voices
like bleeding appeals to the deities of mountaintops
keeps pushing the limit fragmented words of a poem

(xii)

multaque per maestum demens effata furorem
mutilated but sadly demented she blurts out her fury
much she has burked this suffering madness nearing
the other end of the world inescapably the maenad
born of insanity the raging foment of love smitten
can't help herself shifting from red into infrared high
on the helium she smokes returning the shadow to its other
desperate and much the sadly demented her fury fated
keeps going in rounds about the mute cyclopean walls
what intense moments undergoing torment after torment
love letters keep coming back she eats the ink spits
syllables shafts of dead vowels the wounded spite of heart
her face the lacerated mirror of unrequited passion
here here and here the traces of surrender could have
had it all and can never understand why it had to end

chewing the baleful leaf and ranting from highest window
hers are the embolism and aphasia of an enormous error
to have wanted at what a price the solar embrace
bride of the Light eternal never was to be the demented
take her out to the back lot and abandon her to the dark
on her knees rolling in the sullied grasses weeping
stark enmity of fate rocking in sheets of black water

XIV

BOLERO

accused of killing mom fandango dancer
shafts of afternoon death like Bengal flares
denies any association with Rose of Castille
everything is suddenly difficult the languages
one has studied a lifetime and horns lock
the vowels darken a shibboleth to understand
the least line of prose let alone the reasons
why the troubadours went a haunting women
in such dark recesses such lonely distances
a sea between them and the blood they kindled
but to be accused of killing mom the fandango
dancer with his stirrups of cordovan leather
his sombrero what a high thing in the Toledo sun
will we never translate correctly what it was
putting the right foot forward to enter the banquet
ancient bodies conjugated like irregular verbs
in a hispanic tumult of gold and resin sunsets
hush when the purple veil falls and the watchman
puts out the lantern these whitewashed walls
I hear a cornet sound its crimson bright note
in the deeps of Roncesvalles bursting Roland's
betrayed veins and the Saracen hooves pound
a thrill to be mingling sash and satin scimitars
but just how many do you know and how many

can you speak including all the isolated dialects
dyslexia and aphasia to the contrary a mystery
remains embedded in the dry well's fundament
horse-dung colored hills of the Reconquista!
and the fandango dancer tortured for hours
by the Guardia Civil because his name is Lorca
and the darkness that encroaches comparing
this battle to that of Kurukshetra with Arjuna
full of doubts and working his conscience out
in closets full of rose water and musk and chiding
who will come to dispel suspicions all the while
elaborating the original translation emending
monkish errors typographical misconceptions
going to Barcelona in search of the unreal Omegas
and the medieval copyists in their small cells
night and day misunderstanding as much
of latin as possible and the little birds in their
heads fluttering against the dingbat windows
of fettered intelligence can it be we have come
to know so little in a lifetime of devoted learning
and the viola da gamba plying dark arpeggiaturas
in the next room where the fandango dancer
fainted from a set of rubber truncheons dreams
he is at the blood wedding *gitanas* in bodices
with colors borrowed from arroyos of sunrise dust
dance a labyrinthine bolero sweating jewelry
and recollections of the medina and the mosques
of some parchment history about the succession
of imams in far off Babirush adorned with cuneiform
elaborations of the myth of the flood and Gilgamesh
we have only skimmed the mysteries of language
placing the circumflex the acute and the grave
over syllables of quantity to sing them aloud
never quite comprehending the meaning of the words
connecting phonetic aberrations to the god of place
our ignorance is staggering despite the ability
to memorize vedic verb forms in the dawn hour
designing floral compositions for the Beloved

when we cannot even discern her face in the Tavern
is man nothing but a shoulder put to the wheel?
and what of the afternoon lessons about rain
the properties of air the etrurian solemnities
thunder bickering deities two miles from home
and the fandango dancer lapsed into a coma
has visions of muezzins half drunk with love
tumbling out of some repeated oriental tale
gazelles pomegranates elephants talking horses
all brought back to gothic Iberia ca. 700 AD
when the lute and the ruddy fringe of heaven
shaped arabesques in the long indigo afternoons
childhood in grammars of rudimentary semitic
making way for complex substantives in red
weaving in and out of agglutinative periods
everything becomes ever a more difficult berlitz
irreducible sums of colors like women shimmering
in veils the size of ink disappearing into night
false confessions drawn from the tattered quill
admissions to bouts of obsessive lunar ecstasy
implosions of mystical hemophilia and madness
nowhere does it say the human is free from error
his is a monkey life a sequence of imitations
shadow plays of absolutely dumb harlequins
pantomiming the judgment of Paris in old Trojan
so much confusion and role-playing and Bang!
the peripheral characters talking debased Prakrit
come rushing at us all knives and misquoted ire
and the Guardia Civil catholic and hirsute
keep at the fandango dancer who killed his mom

bolero snare drum and bass adagio poco a poco
lamenting he ever swore not to touch her and the song
round and round his demented brain frozen as the skin
she wore in the poem about human error and delusion
sun spots great afternoons in the pandemonium grass
fused to invisible ellipses of the fixed stars at noon
how could it ever be otherwise torment and fever

to have what can never be had and the sheer heights
longing for the figure in the photo processed existence
dizzy to saturation and the world of bees in his head
as he takes the plunge from the dactylic hexameter
into a violent whirlpool of spondees and trochees
successive issues of red and forced ambiguities of love
attempting to revive the twice dead sonata form
as the rhythm slowly picks up monotonous chilling
someone calls out from the screen door behind the alley
where the kids used to play deaf and dead cowboys
dust swirling in immense motes vision a peripheral
stop in the midst of a divine commotion surrounding
the birth of the Other and how many step back gaping
music sheer abundant and physical like the dense hair
of the goddess who patrols the western hemisphere
massive bluish curls spitfire locks beehive permanent
combs of small ivory earring pendants larger than life
elephants that loop through the small cycles of breath
she is having even as the mountain obtains full measure
how total everything is irreversible hugely azure
not enough room to seize the moon in its eclipse
rotations of long dead star stuff sparkling dimly evening
chairs brought on dusky lawns to watch the ivy climb
it is another hour now and the big sound of an orchestra
in the late 19th century mushrooms on the patio
where they are drinking fast and furiously to forget
the forge and the fires and hammers and the anger
what had to happen the instant after the accident
sirens and wrecking crews ambulances of pure speed
mother nowhere in sight the fandango dancer's alibi
holding a highball martini a girl with a vanishing face
I love her how she uses any language with her tongue
like a loom calculating a syntax of unregistered beauty
raptures of synecdoche and splendor of the archaic
to actually speak that way and drive and so narcotic
dreaming it is a day in Elysium obsolete with its marble
intricacies of legend so that everyone is immediate
yet unattached blissed out stoned remote out of touch

drumming from the outer galaxies reaches us now
us humans dedicated to self destruction and exegesis
how can it be we move so rapidly through this medium
at once liquid and sonant all things dissolving in light
the music abrasive and shameless mounting its stairwell
the audience too coming to a chromatic orgasm bolero

could not get him to confess the fandango dancer
sweet reverie of distances near the Guadalquivir
of a remote afternoon the boys all prinked out
in their sailor suits and the drum and fife and
wooden horses jumping up and down sister in
a sky blue pinafore hair in thick braids swinging
and the smell of garlic frying and flies buzzing
green-winged tipping their dreams in the dark
where the patio merges with the unconscious
how swift the civil war would come with metal
and disregard and shoot-'em up everywhere
forbidden to look and silent set up the slate board
with its archaic noun declensions and tio Julio
showing up late with his piano full of Mozart
some said to turn off the radio because the french
and others that a desert storm was on the rise
yellowing the air a thick and the wind stopped
breathing and when we opened our eyes to look
again the house was topsy turvy the Guardia Civil
officers with mustard colored eyes held toys
in their hands barking commands in voices
that seemed to come from *infierno* and sister
tresses undone burst into tears and wrapped
the loyalist banner over her face and stuttered
something like a prayer but they picked her up
and sent her to the moon and in the kitchen
it began to rain thick black drops and frogs
leaping all about and the blur of a disease
that spread through all the rooms including
the one where father took his siesta bundled
inside the Sunday newspaper with its colored

cartoon figures and that was when we noticed
that mom was nowhere in sight and the officers
shifting from room to room they said mom had
contracted tuberculosis and was being removed
to a clinic high above the Alhambra in Granada
where the most Catholic Kings summered in a
heat so abrasive and dense and there was nothing
to be done about it but cry and of course when
evening finally showed up in an umbrella and
strange green spectacles talking about the imminence
of sand and the emptiness we felt in our tiny
sailor suits and going near the broken furniture
afraid to touch the pieces lying there inert so
sad and puzzled to put ourselves to bed with
no one to sing or pray with us and the windows
that looked down on us what a mystery

OK delete the part about the archaic and
strumming a guitar in the key of delta
never will learn the truth about the matter
the distant dusky dense and furious music
as if creeping in through the defiles near
Roncesvalles then abruptly modern and defiant
swaying hypnotically the way the goddess has
scat singing and the mellow tone of the cornet
high above the Pyrenees *sketches of spain*
Joe in the basement stoned of a stifling august
afternoon and the nicomachean ethics opened
to page zero where it says all about how and just
why to do it keeping human the inert mass
within us the swarming unconscious depths
where just about anything can occur like the poem
and the staccato beat persisting in its course
to a deafening crescendo the climax brassy
and resonant thrilling echoing up to the Stars!

XV

LA MER

omnia fert aetas

**the bristling and grandiose sea
when noon is meridian zero the wealth of heat
nothing moves fixed on the glassy surface
sea is less conscious than sky which it meets
sleeping in profound indigo depths
distance is a myth echoed by Narcissus
and there are caves created by the winds
in the solitary recesses of memory
where the only text is a variety of green
like the ivy twined around the temples of Dionysus
grottos inhabited by naiads dead a thousand millennia
whose hair and voices assume the shape of algae
and in the mirage of travel islands abruptly
arise from nowhere in the watery expanse
sheer rock coruscations glittering in the blinding
light steep and black wet as yesterday's eternity
waves rush to meet each other and return
to batter remote shores built on horizons of sand
in the monotonous infinity of the afternoon
when only the sun's massive error seems to shift
ever so slightly toward some wasted Atlantis
a human voice can bear a music of utter longing
the solitude of a voyager lost on the sea of being
even as the world moves within the zodiacal mansion
even as the world drowns in the illusion of water
a water vaster than the history of time
men strapped to barks of night toss to and fro
from tide to tide hearing only the grand susurration
of the undertow which is the moon's terrible sway
and even fainter the small cries of those left behind
those in expectation of a homeward turn
brine mists salt-sting wind burnt skins
dreams woven by the foamy spray languorous**

lying naked on beaches that extend like white shells
around the curving tilt of turquoise
imagining one is home again in the plinth and loom
instead the rush of moaning swells takes the mind
from the body and empties it in the frothy drink
where sinking slowly all its thoughts turn to a verdant dank
"mother! I am coming home, make my bed!"

conch shell sounds eerie shrill summoning
from labyrinthine depths legends of hoary Ulysses
how many times turned his mind wandering storm tossed
thick curtains of fog the brine stung swooned
in palaces lofty and dark of enchantresses and swollen
the enormous sea-sound muffled all clarity and light
his was the embarcadero of a drunken morning
cigarette burns brown rims of a limitless bottle
lowing beast of a hulk dimmed the memory of being a man
shoulder to the plow and traversing the rich loam
dream shifts seeding the archaic world with poppy and asphodel
his dense remove sail spun into a world of golden masks
petty kings jealous and wrathful tossed onto a littoral
scum-green and wild spewing a bitter marine dialect
foaming at the mouth lips cracked and blue
language of hitches and notches and strained hawsers
beneath striated purple thunderhead skies anger
curse of some god to fling him naked to the shoals
a game for pretty girls and treacherous rainbows
intoxicated on the rocks heads up staggering and mysterious
was it the oracle that inveigled him tied by salt ropes
to a splintered mast to listen to the full siren song
maddening his addled brain the more with obsessions
to be one with the Goddess the elusive and violet eyed one
tattooing him with mussels barnacles burning coral
and using him as was her wont crazed underwater
was ever dream more spent in twine of sea grasses
indigo shivered the blistered tongue and roaring
nightmare the color of mercury whipping spume
into the heavens grayish liquids splattered over a canvas

the size of the empyrean and the circling moon
waning divinity eaten by its own wanton tides
maelstrom of the psyche ego-drunk thoughtless
spun round and round the watery vortex
into the deepest gyre of murky darkness
oceanic twin of space voluble churning
nothing to hold no grip just a sense of falling
falling tumbled out of the planetary orbit
into the primordial amniotic gulf
AOI

was then brought and beached vomiting green-froth
finny bits miniscule bone ribbing salt mange
Nausicaa her dancing shadow mini-pleated about his head
so many lives compressed into this liquid moment
shifting in and out and through the sandy shoals
an afternoon out of time only the pounding surf
dense vertiginous whitespray eye memory
walls of angry water rising in massive torrents
sky-colored equal to the solar rotations in strength
taking foam scudded waves across the universe
to where in her circular memory of water Nausicaa
bends picks up the grizzled spouting head in her lap
sings the cooing reverberations tide song so sweet
to wake him into the light again the dry cloud day
where in a drowsy splendor he will revived enjoy
the girl in tension and pull pulse driving moon sounds
and the two will lie forever in sheets of swoon ivy stained
for the life it takes to remember this ever happened
sand and rock and briny foam kisses a rush
darkening membrane of sun setting majesty
when hush of marine breath taints the fainting light
undertow that removes consciousness and

to remember what went before
taking notes or it is sleeping heavier now
islands lapped by slow circulating seas immemorial
sprits and envy was it the guessed whoosh

sky parting to let out still other skies of dark water
drowning to wake and look around if the room
is everything there where it was as a child
pacing words against a fomenting language of tides
talking ceaselessly sand and salt syllables
jabbering you know to somebody inside the wall
a see saw sound in the ear a whisper susurration
spitting jets of stuff out spoiling the map of thought
or to go great lengths to deny descending
watching the memorized hand undergo the current
touching indigo the soft and absent mind
if it's all still the same with age it seems to alter
the lawns and the cataclysm that came after
a citadel high on the sea-cliff abutting the tragic air
bluish clouds come racing down with song
and then pulling the boat to shore the comrades
ropes for faces taut muzzled against the blast
who takes the bride and who jeers taunting
passing the wine skins around drinking deep
like evening with its unmastered dialects
they flounder collapsing drunk on the still hot stones
what a day it was and sleep hard to forget

out far out to the *schwerpunkt* where the waters
become as immense and nothing as space
can be no other course for the dying mind
but set out to sea adrift boundless with only
night and the myriads of stars and their babble
and by day scorched tied by a sheet to the pine
as it rocks and sways to the immemorial rhythms
so many thoughts dispersed among tireless waves
bobbing sweeping diminishing then crescendoing
just as the mind has a way of doing and being
the old things let loose come apart rotting
even words for such things falter disappear
reappear as new sounds in the liquid void
becoming senseless as vedic utterances
in the mouths of dead brahmans

do we ever come back?
do we ever come back to tell what we saw?

and entering that place I saw a great rock submerged
eddying around it the tides and finny things swimming
this was the rock of Distance from which memory derives
its source and clear waters too in springs here and there
crystalline in which bending one could see the gorgeous
face of Narcissus forever bent to drink of his own beauty
ravished and so many others love drunk who now spend
eternity in these waters pining for the shadow of the other
and a bit further where the wrecks of great ships lay
floundering useless and still agitated I saw mariners such
as Sindabad puzzled and in rags reciting from memory
verses from the Shahnamah yet he was not of a person
with substance nor a shade but something of an element
of sheer transparency wavering in the chiaroscuro of
his lore and not far thence was the rusted and massive gate
the entrance some say to Hades far from its terrestrial
reckoning a swaying greenish thing affixed to it many
sucking blind creatures which they say are the straying
last thoughts of men in their delusion and when the gate
swung fully open what lay before me was the vastest
most desolate waste I have ever laid eyes on a veritable
cemetery of the galaxies where lay in pieces the vertebrae of
constellations and dwarf stars the battered hulks of
former suns with their planets loosely floating around
them as if recalling the perfect circles of their childhood
and just inside a host of wailing entities some with names
branded to their emaciated brows others mere wisps
like spermatozoa shifting in the tides and foremost stood
stout Odysseus in his hands were both plow and keel and
intent on sowing furrows with salt he wept bitterly the day
he met Circe and from her was forced to part for in this place
nowhere could he find her who was surely damned as a beast
and not as the divinity he thought her to be and behind him in
shattered mail and greaves Trojan and Greek alike still arguing
bellowing with hoarse and raucous voices for they no longer had

spear or sword with which to cut and not far on a small hillock
was Helen the moon cheeked her face still mockingly beautiful her
tresses matted with gore and blood and small fish ate ravenously
her lips that heroes died to kiss and can I tell too of the dark ravine
the labyrinth and the Minotaur made of several alloys all to ruin
pounding his hooves as if to strike a blaze in this liquid junkyard
and Theseus I recognized for his treachery now a bone ragged
mendicant and poor Ariadne tangled in webs and destroyed
in faith as were so many other damsels and adulteresses and
wives now simpering bitches on all fours pissing ceaselessly
in the mingled eddies and pools where they were left to splash
and flounder and I would tell more but night the eternal has
robbed me of better recollection and I too dazed search for breath
to speak for light to live and as one obsessed keep knocking
on the shattered hulls to peer inside if I could learn more
and take back with me this dream this small white thing
were it not for amnesia consuming my brain and the twelve
types of aphasia the mythical and how I am lost to language
uttering fast and nothing come to rest

toil then those without memory
pushing out to sea the finely carved pine
to navigate the immense unknown
billows and wind squalls to swerve
and rains of forty days and bitter frosts
that make the surface a marble trap
those dedicated to oblivion and loss
doomed never to fully return home
nostalgia of earthlings forced to sail
and to sail forever the sea of being

bittersweet the tide I love
and hark the keening gulls above
their shree shrill cries of abandon
to never know aright
this was my place
adrift
adrift

to the end of time

XVI

THE HYMN TO KALI

**mother of night darkness and crematoria
time and death the unbounded your dance
born of stone you wear garlands of variously
51 or 108 human skulls you have no heart
one of the seven tongues of fire highest reality
devouring everything you remain dark shapeless
essence of your own form you are Great Goddess
the daughter of the mountain the dumb Uma
who scatters everywhere seeds of dissolution
you have no heart and he who night time prowls
in the cremation field wearing only white ashes
muttering a thousand fold your mantra with
matted locks he is the one who becomes a great poet
who Tuesday midnight becomes Lord mounted
on the elephant and sets forth into the world
when you become young again lovely smiling
gesturing with your hands you dispel evil
but can mercy be found in a heart of stone
who has cut off the heads of children to wear
as garlands around your throat kicking the breast
of your master pitilessly who can you be, Mother?
if I call out your name do you ever listen?**

**at the fashion show Heart-of-Stone in tiger skin
and stiletto heel shoes stomps on
disseminating world destruction with every step
blowing kisses to the dozens of decapitated kids
who remain ever devoted blissfully in love with her
because she rejects their love they are more ecstatic
and dance wildly   white ashes**

dispel evil with her smiling hands   Uma
mountain daughter remains dark and shapeless
informing the world with her radiant beauty
tongue lolling out shamelessly scattering seeds
in rapture armed with a sword and noose
violently deep reddish eyes   her roaring
fills all the regions of the sky and devours
the tens of thousands demons she has slain
drunk on the blood of her victims dances
destructive frenzy to destroy the whole universe
in the parking lot turned to a field of corpses
she rages   mmm   stiletto heel shoes
on the chest of her Lord stomping
the more ecstatic   there can be no mercy
without energy matter is dead
Lord Shiva becomes a bawling infant whom she
picks up and breast feeds   how can
we call her Mother ten arms ten legs dancing
born of stone inebriating darkness she can be
the cosmos of love the everywhere of Night
the end of time the very dissolution of time
her hair unkempt her body now young and firm
astride the Lion she   devours all
wearing garlands of 51 or 108 human skulls
can we call her Mother and blue lotuses
in her hands and a sword and a noose so beautiful
her tongue lolling her violent reddish eyes
fangs!   at the fashion show on parade
wearing tiger pelt lissome and   ashes
Tuesday at midnight prowling the cremation yard
become transformed   a great poet
mounting the elephant Lord of the

I was dead to the world I had no life
all about me lay dissolution a wasteland
dead automobiles telephones umbrellas
what god-woman could ever transfer me to heaven
what wit-cup save my mind

no   it must have been something else I did
not the flight to the moon not the
where was I then when love-lost I went astray
wandered the gangetic plain in search of a way
dust I ate and wary of stepping on insects
and naked covered in orange goop
or cowering behind dried tamrisk urinating
reciting mantra tantra hobson jobson
where in the dizzy cosmos was I all those years
several lifetimes wasted in futile avant-garde
posting positions in dada telescope
fame it was lusting after and the fleeting chrome
that girds the head for a moment on stage
LALA what it was all about who knows
did the god-woman once make herself transparent
could I recognize the stone-born one as she walked
down my hometown street all full with gait
swaying imperiously like the elephant
no   it surely was something else I did
nor did I visit the cremation yard Tuesday midnights
to become transformed   a great poet, hunh?
what good all those years leafing Pali manuscripts
puzzling over scribbled 17th century Hindi texts
trying to make it "modern" rubbing alcohol
in all the irregular Vedic verb forms
but why go on   I missed it
I didn't get it   the god-woman
there she was all the time in illustrated lingerie
prinking in strangle-free hose
singing! what a lark her "frozen" song
the radio was full of her and the air for keeps
and magazines numberless skipping through
virtually every page in all colors of the spectrum
LALA what is a god-women doing here and now
transforming and being transformed by electronics
me she doesn't know for she reviles her devotees
devours them chews them up
spits them out like useless black seeds

all over the racing cosmos
so long , Baby   great poet, hunh?

Shakti **the Power raving reddish eyes her**
kicking Baby Shiva   wears the universe
like a ruby embedded in her navel
prancing from black hole to black hole
mistress of dark matter the fling of a
her hair like galaxies of light
certain stories filigree threading through language
taut on a rope suspended between the highest peaks
known to man a rapid succession of skin changes
fires breaking out on the moon
saturn's rings dissolve in instant mercury
to have and have not the waist supple as wind
the air between lives goes too swiftly
maelstroms in the third eye
does not love the children eats them up
wears their skulls variously 51 or 108
garlands swinging above her ponderous breasts
**   another thing**
is the section between the matted locks filth
degenerative tissue howling at the state hospital
where doctor Johnson in frock and rubber hose
baleful leaf passed around hallucinatory vision
mexican peppers rubbed on the tongue
holy jeezus! to confess to such crimes
reducing the Deccan to a plateau of white ash
leaving in her wake the assassinations of hindu ***sants***
poets enmeshed in the jungle of dravidian syntax
going up and down through the lacunae
in the sundry chronicles of Sri Lanka
blue monky gods atomized by her glare
insensate to all human passions she makes do
with the terrific and ruddy insanity
of the necrophiliac and the nymphomaniac
how she moves mysteriously through the zone
infinitesimal that separates orgasm and despair

taking in her skirt of a thousand writhing serpents
whole oceans boiling tides steaming brains!
if she opens the jewel box   Beware!
ghoul and fiend poisoned asps spring forth
cunning now youthful with firm body
enticing with her smile of pure abracadabra
induces four-faced Brahma to his knees
all ten directions go up in the holocaust blaze
of a hundred thousand atomic bombs
she's left standing in her violent Sanskrit miniskirt
hands on hips sticking her great lolling tongue out
it's time for everyone to die
forget the story about salvation and paradise
she doubles the size of infinity
***Shakti* the seething end term of the cosmos**
why weren't we better people
***Shakti* matter without energy is dead**
why did we let the years go by so fast
why was the last so lonesome a night
and then the small proof of nothing
but the echo of the vortex

to Myth turning reddened shafts of purulent light
can we ever and the massive moment when recognized
for who she is not the dallying young Uma fresh from
the mountain dew strolling down walnut street a century
ago a parasol of human eyelids turning in her hand and that
flirtatious winsome half-smile inviting king and pauper
alike to kiss her Lotus Feet can we ever but the strident
nightmare dressed in torn tiger pelt ten arms and legs
how many heads and the clotted masses of thick black
hair tossing this way and that dancing on baked drum skins
garlands of human skulls knocking against her breasts
a radio going off somewhere in the galaxy with a music
of clicks and echoes and tattoos and something about
the human condition the enigmatic only partially learned
the little understood as the ballet of corpses resumes its
movement adagio ma non molto yes at that very moment

when we do Durga puja and the slums of resistance and
acrimony and the seven hundred establishments of hell
open up their awnings and her tongue extends to the depths
licking us in dreams sulfuric and abysmal when we think
to return to childhoods designing perfect cities only to
want to bomb them out of existence yes at that very moment
when destruction is the only pleasure remaining and she
astride her lion of the moon painting with bloody hands
the pastorals of Radha and Krishna is it the verb to "be"
or is it the verb to "fuck" which is the most important and
yes at that very moment and the famous blackness spreads
over the remaining worlds and there is nothing you can do
and she embraces the mountain reducing it to rubble
and the solar mansion opens its bright brassy portals
and voices emerge contradictory and fulminating reciting
great poetry from all the lost languages but indifferent
to universal suffering Kali resplendent and awful in this
moment of horrific awareness makes herself available
to none rejects all suitors lovers husbands paramours and
aggravation and annihilation of the English-speaking planet
like a typhoon full of raging waters she roars devastatingly
through the Temple and renders it null and void no more
godhead or supreme Truth just the enervating mind-end
of the beginning of everything all over again

loosely put and dressed in flimsy rags
the god-women at the back door begging
despite layers of grime her face stupendously
radiant the all-bright of sheer transcendence
dare we let her in the house across the sacred lintel
no need she walks in all sans souci as if long familiar
with every room floor stairway *"this is my house"*
she declares in her emphatic beast voice
"this is the house of Catastrophe"
this is toxic game a toss of the bones to read
our finality the infinities within Infinity
all blue rushing like a whirlwind from her nostrils
and she stands there throbbing ecstatic

talking snake talk and rubbing white ash
all over her naked body and kicks Baby Shiva
one last time really lets him have it
BOOM   out go the lights

XVII

(APOCRYPHA/FRAGMENTA)
the aggravated futility

this is the part where seeking a heaven
    and none is to be found unless in dreams
the scant remembered and aching because
of the half-recalled words oracular
    divine at times always enigmatic
"only the two of us left" and looking
at the stretch of big water as it curves
mysteriously outwards toward a horizon
      tumbling down the sand slope
to lie there together on the beach as if
it were the "old times" half a century gone
and nothing had happened in between
      just the monotonous series of deaths
that mark the relentless passage that
defines this brief season of light and rain
   as life the culmination of error and
painting and if we could see all over again
the buildings darkening in their interior

the palace of Minos where light is spared
   and one moves as if in a shifting hour
where nothing is fixed and voices manifest
secret and wandering declaring the nothing
which is to be had by opening a door
                    lost epics
the list now illegible of all the gods and

goddesses   a white hand
      descending from the cloud loom
sprinkled ashes and water
                    the mingling of names
formless disembodied sprites from the mind
        depart   and in secret chambers
the accounting of urns and casks
how much wine how much grain
        and from Egypt the big prowed ships
in their bellies hidden even newer
      deities bearing seals and spears
        it is for this that writing
transforms the air
          that singing and longing

speak ill of no one
lest it come back on you

and this is the part where we divide
the map collection the lawns the skies
the long avenues of summer where we
waited for the Friend
who was coming slowly with *the* book
to spend hours in the reading of it
imagining that we are no longer here
no longer the ones who are reading
to whom has been imparted this shred
of light this miniscule entry to otherness
and find ourselves suddenly darkened
inebriated raving something new
something just discovered about
the heavens yes the gyrating
mechanics of fire   the
invisible winches and levers that
transfer us from the body
            who can be talking
in the next room?
what voice is unraveling   delphic

code shades
the distance to

whispering in the eaves falling asleep
to be conscious listening
symbols   allusions   chimerae
to reinvent the sentence to reinvent syntax
suffocating heat   isolation
thunder in a sky like a blank piece of paper
instead of pausing   for ink
more words a description
of when angel was at the door
impenetrable night
chirring   leaves
and asked for just a teaspoon's worth
to make it worthwhile   descending
from the seventh sphere
regroup thoughts   flight of days
the bad deeds of conscience
insomnia you could see it in angel's
famished eyes leagues of sand hovering
above an atmosphere threatening tempests
counting backwards from the gate of heaven
to the still point where number
loses category silent distant
the purely remote of an archaic
unintelligible myth
call that the   Muse

instead of piecing the missing parts together
and placing the verbs at the end and translating
it as if it were just yesterday you had to go ahead
and create ab ovo the syntax rubbed against silence
signals illusions the head winds of pages rushing
into a vortex of memory what could be darker than
this mythical complex of springs and running waters
and mirror images of one tortured by self doubt and angst
and the running text below which kept adding footnotes

in red ink and the supply of nominals in a totally
cryptic manner leading one nowhere but astray or
adrift in a panoply of words suggested from the hoard
found underneath where the lists of now defunct gods
ran on and on in a crypto-sumerian dialect confined
now to the hill uplands of Transoxania and the innuendos
about the Ur-hero and his ax and the woman who suborned
him a plague on the lot and looking for references from
a much later epoch kings with gilded masks queens by
day whores by night the legendary apocalypse that
happened just next door when the fighting began
after a riot over the abducted Helen and of the many
Helens which was She none to remember exactly who
or why just a snub-nosed little bitch in silk finery
and naughty underchosies and an Egyptian flare for
seduction in abandoned movie lots you know and the
great et cetera that follows this apocryphal reading
going on and on you just couldn't stop brooding about
the past the historicity of such unclassifiable data worsened
by an inability to stick to grammar rules seamless errors
the time was 1945 downtown Los Angeles the movie was
"Leave her to Heaven" there were fires in the Baldwin Hills
and much was troubling that winter and the long train ride
to ice country frozen rails steel hard skies clouds brim
with catastrophe and blinding the white and nebulous
future hanging clothes out to freeze and listening carefully
to the message of the mourning doves despite the orthography
in the snow and claustrophobia of deathlessness squandered
youth in the slopes always nostalgia and longing missing
mother absconded who knows to what cemetery to waste
away phthisic in her floor length embroidery and wasn't
home a house anymore but signals allusions and chimerae
trying to set it all down in some kind of orderly but
how many attempts sketches half-starts unfinished magna
opera can one fit into a life the disappointment countless
words misused other directed poorly understood lilacs
in the longest sleep and just a step away from the tomb

isn't the text a problem linear Alcatraz
as far as the bay can fling its mists reading
between the bridges a syllogism for matter
darkening is not the worst it can bring
but isolation standing up to the boulders
of criticism while waves salty peaked shake
the limbo of memory up vallejo street and
down green street in search of the omicron
some bitter little antidote from chinatown
spreading between oranges and upside down
failed to read aright the judgments in fever
like windows through which meaning flies
nothing to do but underscore the keening
birds circling above the limitless paragraph
ominous darkening the parallel bars' stain
apocryphal disjunctions side by side with
girlfriend in her latest cuneiform dimension
emerge shapeless between docks the harbor
within us the listing deity white hands froth
cannot overcome the speech defect prayer
attitude beside the self abject and petty
falling from the palms secret meanings
elusive as the eleusinian response nights
when the moon is missing heat rings a
sentiment that all is over the situation
fleeting images of before dying wisps
of cold hair descending into the arroyo
where whiplash and tongue-job wash
syntagma of fire smaller words snatches
of a greater light a

emissions   fault lines   apocrypha
"by the grace of Ahuramazda all that we did"
immense distances overcome in a fleeting minute
we are returned to our place of origin
burning hospitals numerals beyond reach
rings of Saturn blackening in the trophies of sleep
do we imitate the stop-watch in our desire to "have"

what was never ours in the first place
waiting on that summer avenue for the Friend
for *the* book to open up with its prodigious
and illegible prophecies
the heart is all a monsoon a storm
rains and darkening afternoons of no return
brooding on the missed appointment
on the failed promise on the mistaken letter
on the forgotten illusion the chimerae indwelling
when we cannot give up our egos when we
this blank scroll what is it meant to say
that the islands we were destined to visit
have all gone away that the Myth in its stark outline
is a mirage of desert cities and palaces
it is silk next to the skin
and mouths like ripe fruit forbidden to kiss
and the Moorish tannery where colors open
under a black and archaic sun
it is not for us to remember anything now
the decades which collapse into minutes
thinking to understand what has no meaning
staring at photographs where the faces like glyphs
give no clue as to the identities hidden there
writing daily to recover what is irreversible
the time lapse of horizons of ancient sand
correcting the often truncated sentence to no avail
reinventing syntax or destroying it repeatedly
not making literature but shibboleth
the frequent poem about the redhead
whose music is a total dissonance in the Hour
was it a mistake to check in at the Hotel Europa?
what was the effort to continue "creating"?
writing daily to recover what is irreversible
here here and here we thought to strike "it"!
the sun's chaotic error kept circling the mines
where the ancients excavated for memory
and yet here we are today impoverished and
ink-stained blotting out unwanted words

uselessly asleep at the driving wheel
careening from misfortune to misfortune
hoping tomorrow they will have a cure
wanting desperately to understand to "get it"
what will the next letter in the alphabet be?
will it stand for "ruin"?
in whose hospice are we languishing today
how can it be that the dead in their checkered suits
keep coming back in the extra month of sleep
offering us their hands to write with
waking to realms of indecipherable stones
markers on the route to bad literature
to philosophical discourses about the *nous*
when will the books of genesis that Mozart wrote
come to full transduction
it is all around us the relic of the Flood
on the left hand side of the circle
the distance is equal to that of the right hand side
and in between gapes the yawning abyss
which is the bottom of time
whatever turns up in written form
whatever is described in so many words as "life"
whatever given a minus sign is the suchness of truth
why do we keep relegating this very tale
to the midden heap where the apocrypha lie
like so much residue reduced to ashes
sifting through them looking for one word
that makes sense anymore
"I had nothing coherent to say
            I had no language"

XVIII

THE MAHABHARATA RECONSIDERED

> ***"The heralds, infatuation and illusion,***
> ***sing my praises, bards my limitless faults"***
> ***"—she went without her body"***
> **Sur Das**

where is my winged chariot,
where are my war wounds?
difficulty compiling choosing refining versions
which can be definitive? lotus and trampling elephants
red eyed demons paper-eating flying wildly
and swaying melon breasted gopis in a trance
the names of the Lord OM
recondite in jungles of sperm and sweat
what criteria to adopt always shifting points of view
mass of molding documents nothing precise no directives
only memories of conversations silverfish scurrying
over dog-eared palm leaves boomerangs mantras
who said what to whom buzzing of discordant languages
discarded syntagma lush undergrowth thousands of years
and the brothers still arguing scheming full of envy and spite
gambling drinking whoring
and what conversations! among them a deity prowled
smell of jasmine hibiscus garlands thrown around the neck
some divine plan afoot and the blindness
either by birth or by intention and the cheating
angry seers laying multiple curses and the sun
his effigy and offspring hidden in the dust
churls and high-minded princes with nose-rings and tattoos
among them a god child-like and secretive guile deceit
it depends on which century you think you're in
which dialect you're struggling to unravel
fisticuffery boomerangs spitfire
rivers flowing deep and wide from which lotus-born Brahma
the four-faced and goddesses tantalizing and firm have sprung
and you wonder in which epoch the aborigines exist

nose-boned and hunkering behind putrid underbrush
waiting for the kill chattering empty vowels
or the monkeys divinely inspired in the trees looming
bound for Sri Lanka with dream spells of saliva
and what conversations!   child Arjuna aiming
his infallible arrow at the eye-painted bird target
"snap outta that!" mumbo jumbo voodoo vedic pidgin
drawing large red circles in the dirt
to call down unwilling Indra king of the gods
whose days are spent lazing in powder blue Pontiac ca. 1956
does me good to write like this reduced to shreds
the poem about ten miles long in one direction
and maybe fifteen miles in the other direction
unnatural disposition of bonzes growing fetid in the noonday blaze
chanting chanting eyelids burnt off blind to the world
and when they're done talking all outta their heads
and asking for more club soda and gin fizz
and on this side of the barrier reef the kauravas
a hundred strong full of grit and deception
and on the other lined up a mere handful the pauravas
with mother Kunti like a blade shining in the light
whole lotta roaring and jumping up and down
caterwauling spear flinging and   boomerangs!
bringing back the heads of some of them and others
lying there in pools of sapphire blood   ah Lord!
supine or erect what does it matter
the radio is loud and wide broadcasting blow by blow
and as far off as sumeria the god Varuna half drowned
reemerges to report with deaf fingers of the dread battle
that awful afternoon in Kurukshetra when Duryodhana
on his knees finally got it for what he'd done to Draupadi
trying to disrobe her that day in the Assembly Hall
shame and fie on the lot of them in their rusted trucks
and waving banners depicting the victory of the color red
what a wind blew that night and in the marsh whimperings
beheading all those sleeping kids   more boomerangs!
great hobson jobson mantras   Krishna's conch shell
blowing one intense clear note across the universe

only memories of conversations
flitting shadowy figures on the large Indonesian screen
each is every one or none is the other so many dialects
profusion of inherent vowels of unaccented syllables
confusion of grammatical gender of retroflex consonants
divagations of apophony twelve kinds of aphasia
linguistic diseases proliferating in the Deccan
where the sea washes its warm tides against the cliffs
shall we then to old Mumbai and crown the queen of pop?
shrill voices warbling emotions ancient as the moon
"what's bitter but love's sweet memory" **SHANTI**
and up from the Dravidian thickets NataRaja on his wheel
comes sowing havoc and destruction laying low whole jungles
in an atomic instant and bejeezus all the folk look up
to see the cosmos delivered of its matter
for a million light years which is only a matter of instants
everything revolves evolves comes around again
and shattering to smithereens comes together again
one whole consistent vibrating particle of sound Yes!
homeopathic remedies to no avail ayurvedic claptrap
opened wounds torn sutures deities moaning on their cruppers
is there a doctor in the House?
and whose shadow bluish tinctured dripping in the mirror
is that manifesting all ghostly twilight screened
"when he sees me in everything and sees everything in me"

what conversations!
unfolding the mass of moth-eaten documents
unraveling the skein of tales half-truths outright lies
empty as a drum excoriated and left to dry in the sun
the skin of memory withered and desiccated faintly
tattooed by years of interpolations and translations
until the thing hanging from the tree limb
surrounded by thick clusters of gnats and green winged flies
that thing shaking ever so slightly as if whispering
to the afternoon breezes that thing almost transparent
and weightless that thing is memory itself repository
of a hundred thousand unwritten histories and languages

touch it and it crumbles to dust particles so minute
go back to sleep dear heart wander no more this flat earth
underneath where dreams are spun put the head
and when your eyes are closed decipher then the rock
read aloud the countless fabrications of archaic myth
raveling as you do the punctuations of thought
senseless meanderings in the grammar book of time
Monkey! pray tell what is the cause of grief?
look in the maps of water in the florid designs of air
are there places of pleasure and pain hidden there
are there ascensions to heaven or descents to hell
described in vivid detail in those vast mappings?
looking up from my little bed what do I discern
but the hollowed shells of deities who have abandoned
their definitions to become all ethereal as One
they have transcended the origins of the body
leaving us to do battle with the shapes of ire and envy
cleaving from the one its firm trunk and from the other
its abundant and beautiful head of hair AOI
vapors scintillating in the instant of pure dissolution
once names and geographies rich and pornographic
supple identities of paramours and veils and tombs
for whom we die for and inscribe great poems
that involve centuries of longing and seeking for what
Monkey! pray tell what is the cause of sorrow?
writing everything that has ever been experienced
translating it interpreting it misunderstanding it
never comprehending what so impassions the intellect
why it ever falls short of itself in a yellow mass
do we appeal to the diacritic or summon the circumflex
and put everything in quotation marks or italics
to emphasize what remains enigmatic
do we hold the mirror to the script to misread it
to make it waver and turn liquid and run through space
does the end of the day bring us to grief
another twenty four hours spent in vain
biting our knuckles regretting the parried sword
that has brought the enemy down again and again

shadow plays performed incessantly to explain what
AOI

how many clouds have passed since we last met
and shall we ever meet again you on that border and
I on the opposite shore hands aloft waving weaving
intricacies of wind and bloom the flowering of breath
in me you transient and insubstantial fleeting as unseen
air puffed over the heads of dandelions in you me however
wavering weaving transient as ash dispersed over the Himalayas
we are come to naught to silences beyond silence unmarked
as space in its inception remains unmarked nameless
circles circling the Wheel of birth and death that turning
gives us light and turning returns us to darkness and for all
that we seem to remember conversations in water and air
hands forming constellations of myth and childhood distances
encumbered only by the shadow of one another traversing
the great road that wends over the hill into the vast dry plain
where imagined cities shimmer for an instant only then revert
to ant heaps pocking the arid terrain of the archaic planet
clouds shuddering above changing shape ceaselessly becoming
now fire now cold now longing now nothingness of sleep
seem to remember something else an argument a bickering
over what a coin a girl a wager to learn something else
to overcome the body and its sources to merge somehow
the other with its other in a labyrinth of mirrors and light
coming and going calling out to the hollows and receiving echoes
back legends shreds of a tale scraps of a recollection about
when there was a great fight and either side weeping and
menacing night starless and perfect to wind its shroud around
the multiplied husks shells exoskeletons dried pods blown
like a dust of migraines in all directions reddening denser
than before when there was the other tale to tell and the seers
who came down the mountain with the unknown one she
in white raiment who stepped like the moon across the vast
a riddle of otherness to touch a flake a petal of albescent
material such a thing and the brothers you and I in formation
opposites to each other yet knowing which of us would speak

and which silently would take and the quarrel that would ensue
and heights and depths flowing and surging like an invisible
water issuing mysteriously out of the oracle's mouth a silken
thread linking rust to the aching in the heart what else is there
now the countless clouds that have passed since we last saw one
another and the countless more before this will occur again

frightful vision of mendicant gods before them
the enormous red of the warring planet shaking
like mica or shale in the full sun blaze of noon
brother cutting brother down trajectories of flaming
explosives bursting in the limpid and terse air
cloudless yet thunder roaring sky shattering silence
into its dissonant vowels and blood shed from leaves
consonants in formless clusters choked in the throat
as igneous arrows fly into one eye after another
and the ensuing blindness projects its universality
over the tenebrous and interminable afternoon
should Monday ever come again will the wash be done
will men in pressed cloth board trains to do business
there must be better things in our human nature
to obtain than ***this*** **meat quivering despair and tears**
was Kennedy a coward to back down from Cuba
will the end come as a heart shaped mouth yearning
or as a maleficent firecracker the size of our galaxy?

and Markandeya said
came forth the legions of chariots elephants and horses
in array magnificent to behold and not far off the peahen
danced to entice its mate making a drumming sound
a coterie of gods weary of rolling dice in Kapilavastu
came to peer over the brocaded edge of their cloud-home
and beheld illustrious mortals clash among themselves
making of bright day a furious night thick with missiles
that carpeted the life-giving air and nostril choking dust
nor were the ladies exempt from the bloodbath but endured
insult rape and ignominious wounds throughout the body
being dragged as chattel into the steaming jungle

and by twilight a fog of horror hovered over the plain
jackals and birds of prey made feast of human entrails
brains spilled over shields oozing into the clotted earth
everywhere the rent cries and lamentation of mankind
the ruddy blur of sun sank slowly as if in shame in a horizon
no longer visible for the enormity of the crimes committed
that day was as no other in the annals and maimed bards
scarce had voice to find rhyme and meter to fit the catastrophe
"when he sees me in everything and sees everything in me"

SHANTI OM

XIX

CONFESSIO AMANTIS

"I wolde go the middle weie
And wryte a bok between the tweie
Somewhat of lust, somewhat of lore,
That of the lasse or of the more"
John Gower

"Honest, Officer, I only meant to touch her,
that's all, please"

my first galactic girlfriend she's the one
in the scottish plaid pinafore and large gold safety pin
an excellent example of the feminine declension
she was the perpetrator of small sacrileges
risen from the Dictyean realm her face flush pink
the origins of celestial body mechanics a smile
darkly emerging from oblivion's bleak hotel
to hold her heaven spread its diaphanous down
and what else could matter but the moment
of the dance when lights out the song ethereal
wafted us to the world before the pyramids
where oceans and planets and jungles merged

not a thought existed only tingling the strand of hair
on the cheek teasing setting the trance in motion
soft perfume striations of ultramarine light a fog
of intentions extinguished the bicameral mind
apollonian and dionysian fused into an orchestra
of muted horns strings and massive distances
barely aware of movement the feet shifted steppes
feathery puffs of heat the sweat breakout clutching
tightly to the breast the reorientation of existence
mythiform dreams faint tint of ether globes of helium
the gradual disappearance of red becoming blank
the whitest pale imaginable skin melting like snow
drifting into colonies of remote tropical orgasm
to never wake again green somnolence buzzing

situated at the corner of 1st avenue and 2nd street SW
Webber & Judd's drug store & suspended from the entrance
above the sidewalk the four-faced clock like the faces
of Brahma directing the traffic of that busy bus-stop
in all quarters of the universe one had but to wait
for the moment to ring for the world to recommence
and in the back room colognes and cherry cokes
afternoon date with cashmere sweater and fake pearls
twilight in eyes seagreen plundered by endlessness
a longing that can never be defined and growing up
finds so much more involved with wind-tossed tresses
bright lip coloring and scanty in and out see through
the atomized perfection of a foreign scent and shapes
of pure distance undulating through magazine pages
arrived from far off Krete mysterious of small words
evoking something ineffable and terrible at the same time
wearing nothing more than the imagination of skin
and the wild hair that belongs to the empress Theodora
in the Annunziata position in some wayward fane
nostrils flaring lids half-shut mouth parted inviting
the god who created her to undress her with a kiss
breathlessly narcotic a library of lush voluptuousness
the secrets of the body yet be recognized and cataloged

**fluted winds bearing aloft the discarded pink lingerie
musk and libidinous alcohol clouding the profundities
of her deathless eyes in which an insane Jerusalem lists
the ungovernable hypothesis of her rampant sexuality
pure myth and delusion of the mortal error in its sun
towers of knowledge turned to dust by her whims
evidence of a carnal world tropical and swarming
in the incarnadine polish of her finger- and toenails
reckless in the way she walks utter snake of deceit
she's no one you'd ever introduce to the home folks
in shady byways dirty alleys behind the lilac hedges
she ditches her immortal shadow for a fool's embrace
in the back rows of darkened movie theaters abandoned
she flings herself in the arms of depraved truant Lords
symbolizing her touch with a dozen briar pricked roses
endlessly rutting doll-like in her porcelain perfection
she laughs off worldly wisdom flinging her burnished locks
sticking a tongue out lolling and wagging the biggest tease
pretending to own the alluring resonances of Echo
hers are the hiss the buzz and the shh of impure sounds
she is Mind in all its chromatic and unending plurality
for she is one troubling multiform thought a noetic city
she is intellect razed to the ground green turpentine
celestial vagabond protean innocence in a seashell
making music of a mercurial syntax all loose ends
nothing that ever begins a shifting red envelope of breath
looping through the interstices of emotional finales
spreading a perpetual haze over just and right thinking
ultimately the drum dum-dum of a tattooed obsession
writing the syllable of her name over and over in helium
goddess of tautology and infernal boredom sex-play
kinematic incandescence in a ballet of ruptured organs
frenzy of silent consonants to enunciate the ineffable
shoo-shoo diptych cast in abstract oils and acrylics
splattered cosmically over a canvas of dead neurons
can she never be other than the fixed infatuation of infinity
dappled naked light years of forever coming into being
perpetuum mobile pornographicum doo-wop shhboom!**

I confess that I am forever ensnared raptured to death
with her who is whatever you name it blitz & holocaust
the functionless toy-box exploding forever in the brain
to have at her to snatch the goal before it finishes to be
encircled by the moon of her ninety nine diphthongs
to be inside out within her entrails budding madness
planting symbologies of extra planetary rotations
wearing her cosmetics her jewelry her flaming underclothes
going up and down the heavenly stair with an empty birdcage
knowing I am lost to have her condemned by society
for reciting ad nauseam love letters I have sent her
all returned unread crossed out crumpled and illegible
why am I confessing this to you Officer I only touched
that soft unnamable spot a couple of times harmless
she flips out when I draw near with my magnifying glass
with my electric scissors with my hot tongs and teeth
why is it am I so obsessed with this amalgam of stardust
and moondrift this lunatic double vision mirror image
of my narcissistic self in the cross hairs of a lost illusion
intangible as all passions are it is not love it is not anything
like love I suffer because I have never been in love with her
only the devouring end-all sensation of a violent itch
purulent nerve bongs going off up and down the spine
I wanna go *yadda ta dadda yadda ta dadda* inside her
and then as the One we were forever meant to be Wild!
read together in perfect unison the Brahma Sutra sotto voce
being inextricably the suchness of our own singularities
a-swoon in her massive hair dying of her pizza-red lip gloss
shaking with the quatrains that riddle to excess her memory
how can we ever be other than the Other we seem to be
I am a shadow vomiting everything I ever knew about her
it is not love it is not anything like love it is Repulsion
it is the downside of occidental philosophy the master negative
through which one perceives the universe from its conclusion
backwards into the multiple still frames of instamatic red
which is the color she endows to her trillion devotees
and I am the chosen of so many myriads the one to die
first in the stampede out of the Temple of Isis ah Glory!

I am with her and she is with me in Webber & Judd's drugstore
the four faces of Brahma are witness to our celebration
we share one table one chair one glass one plate one straw
unidimensional in our complete otherness no one sees us
what we are is the ripple in the glass the heat in the ice
the cigarette left burning on the edge of time the smoke
which can never return and she that draws the invisible
through the vast emptiness we leave after our love-making
it is one day past the Monday of 1956 and there is nothing

drool synergy magma insane buzz of moths around the lamp
I confess to shadowing her on the porches of Attica and on to
the Ionian shores where Thales sat and opined about the then
known Kosmos star stuff ether fire water air substances and
earth hidden behind a panoply of rusted weapons leftovers
from the Trojan debacle I sniffed her out of the tamarisk and
stalked her night day in and out of music venues used car lots
hotel basements hospital cafeterias trick shops and finally
cornered her behind a shut down 5 & 10 store outside of
Damascus and if I touched her there Officer if I lay a single
finger on her I swear to Venus it was just that the slightest
graze of the fingertip I didn't mean to make her howl I didn't
want her to go on all fours barking like a diseased Maenad
I wanted her to be all soft like cushions or lush carpets contours
and undulations perfumes of night musk of oriental decay
not this effervescent post puberty madness rabid and making
like a dog on a fire hydrant and I confess only to watching
her dissolute and dissolving in the thousand degree heat
of her disorientation No I didn't lay a hand on her and
it was never anything like love that made me do it No it
was aggravated and forlorn an absence of humanity a
detachment from error Yes more like resigning the self
to the high noon sun shedding the layers of ego and desire
distant from any shade lidless blind to the mind's purulent
wound from which the multiple worlds of illusion and history
trickle down the skin No it was never love never only the obsession
to read and write and destroy what has been written and blank
Yes to be blank omniscient dead senseless to oncoming light

to breath uninformed shapeless drifting drifting drifting

**next door to Webber & Judd's was the bookstore
of Lucy wilder gateway to the universe of so-called
literature modern library editions of Chaucer Dante
Rabelais Gibbon Joyce and Faulkner and around
the corner on the same block was the imposing yellow
granite Plummer Building of the Mayo Clinic with
its impressive lobby dark any time of year and busy
with practitioners of Aesculapius and the multitude
of sick from all quarters of the universe and across
the street was the 14 floor Kahler Hotel and beneath
linking those two structures and other hospitals as well
a mysterious marble tunnel haven in winter for lovers
to get out of the cold and play kissing games and that
was just what we did enraptured and innocent then
bewildered but certain that this was the force of Love
the commanding force of the galaxy the secret kindling
of the fire that makes music**
*pulled back the quiver and let fly the shaft
directly to the heart it flew and made target*
**in front of the county courthouse was a civil war cannon
and down the gentle slope across the street up a bit
was the grand sandstone public library with its large
reading room and great windows all about that let in
the sun whilst one studied at one of the tables surrounded
by multiple volumes bound in green or red leather of
encyclopedias and dictionaries and numerous books
of reference covering all fields of learning
distracted by the presence of one another looking up
too frequently from the pages of the latin grammar
her face like a valentine or so it struck his fancy to be
how brief seemed the afternoons when yearning was afoot
what mysteries were invoked by the merest touch of
skin against skin and both went back to where shelves
and shelves of books hid their bodies from view and
thence lip met lip and kissing profound to take away
the very breath dizzying between titles such as *The Loom***

of Language **or** ***Modern Psychology*** **and thereupon**
recovered for a minute or two but then went back
and delved in the Secret
never again was the labyrinth so intricate

they called it "going steady" the first intensities
that drained the senses and caused the blood to flare
mooning idiotically over the proverbial soda
never for an instant wanting to be out of touch
with the inane the insane provoked to acts of
legend held sway and echo and her Muse
and the riot of small deities who prick and itch
thus do I confess to have been a victim
and from that time Officer have been lured
by the sirens' song and gone out of the mind
seeking to touch what can never be possessed

"For every man his oghne wone
After the lust of his assay
The vice or vertu chese may"

XX

THE MIASMA

Κλυταιμνήστρα
has forever flown the ancient mess a forlorn
adjective subject to blank periods of excess
the thickened plot the cloud smitten ovarian
flight in what subjunctive mood stress howls
wildly like hair in arrears mirrored in pools
checkered a life spent fuming outside the gate
flimsy cloth tattered the demon panting his
own out to flatter her into criminal postures
heading a cast of Argive minions too flunked
to shape any kind of future in the alloy mines

or simply putting the accent on her mind wows
the audience stunted by evenings of despair
pouring their wine into caskets and greaves
once the proud gear of dust mired warriors
now he comes back the king ruddy with gore
with his little Cassie off the ship up the hilly
path gravel strewn and white by moonlight
to the palace what a greeting tables packed
with sweet meats viands custards flaring pies
goblets of heady booze ichor thick like black
ink downed and then to the bath half plowed
no wits left to be seized as the gods would have
it by fate's dotty little hand ax gripped and
there you have it blood outing it like water
through a sieve so goes his soul the damned

(variation 1)
the short the eager and the feather cracker
bats flying thick as gnats at the wall
stories like doors feathered for safeway
while most tales flake mica densely
other trials flue fake gemstones dank
sublorned the idiot paces heaving stones
the ball the beaver and the future creaker
flats crying flayed morosely dumb steel
widgets humped by bathing flails ahoy
seasweeps gill ferns cresting violently
til noon drunks chipping at the moon
distill yet another history full of feats
featured in the animated version for krill
thunk dumping shafts of red twill crap out
crepe papered the sill's battered window
weeps her lust hubby downed by bumstead
mortar skulls the bull as hunk and an ether
breath foils the failed screwstump driver
unless breasts torn from flames smoke
rerun endless looping carnivorous domes
et dit dot wadda ladda merde moo shoo

(variation 2)
Sweetums, come home!
don't leave me in the dumps to wail and moan
uncle Aegisthus done paint me up with war-black
saying bitter times gonna come coiled and frilled
like a flapper doo-wop shunting the hose up
my legs a finery of nylon seamless as the sun's rupture
and dreaming all moon-beamy smarmed afternoons
on end drinking this swill poison and hit my veins
all hard to the spine up I go erect as a queen
you just say the word and I'll do the old Goat song
tragedy from the start palaces like labyrinth
night dark even at noon thick curtained and sealed
like a jailhouse in Albuquerque so's not to let
the light in that reveals sinners us all
hymn-spouting with the dead organ grinder
and his little Monkey scarlet nosed bobbing
up and down the Attic escalator
or so says Aeschylus in his crupper
cupped to the brim by acid and taped lies
dulcet tones never scored

(variation 3)
pale I am the wan blanched frail the little
lunar thing spent whiter than sacrificial stones
lying all scattered hair loosed to the winds
who'll ever say that's me the flitting image
willow thin in the reflecting glass who'll
ever say they knew me in the grass and dark
of a night far off in Sparta daughter of the swan
Leda flirted and betrayed by the big Man-god
ah that was the other life sore times a gone
born and sacked and dragged over the waves
fit for a night of anger in the cellars of the heart
just so tired of the play strutting and ranting
on this paper stage tie a sheet around him while
he's in the tub and stab the life out of him nasty

cocker that he was bringing that Trojan vamp
all outta her mind too the rave and say what's
that song upstairs is that the Erinyes practising
their chorus for the final act when I paler yet

(variation 4)
what a romp the both of 'em according to Homer
calls it the miasma the gore haunted night curse
o' the Atreids mummers decked out in death's
worsted flannels and fired up for a slaying song
moon light sonata pig trotters bladder wart
eye brightener you name it called into play
the broth simmering in the brain a plot to ploy
fumous discord fidgeting little deities pulling
hair by hair out of the rattling heads mown
like flowers of grief all over Persephone's lawn
crimson eddied the fateful stream running through
it the floss and scrum she'd a pulled it out had
the chance to give a life away and the winds
that didn't move the boats and poor little Iphie
boy that made her cry and angry man was she
ever waiting for him to come home one night
top of the stairs with an arsenal to bleed an army
the oaf swilled to the chops dumber than a rock
he plunges into the vat and gets it just like that
all numb the curtains thicken and plead

(variation 5)
c'est triste la gloire fanée les mémoires anéanties
pourquoi suivre ce chemin de rochers et pluie
there's no room left in my heart just a waste
of nettles and sky blown heather colorless fade
night swarm of silent furies down-sweeping
into the mind's bleak atrium where diddle Iphie
used to play suppliant roaming hades now
an orphan blasted by the storm's aggressive mutiny
all them sailors and captains buckling swords up
for the kill on some vast cliff land a hundred years

from here just ‘cuz Menelaus took it in his gut
to claim Helen for his the smarmy bastard
and I’m just a floor of empty rooms unlit and
windows where my body dries wasting for a day
when sunless the tragedy will have its gloat
gravel minded with cities of sand and grit
to fall towers bastions harems crenellated walls
the whole smithereened to bits tooth and nail
cups of bile I ooze and pour the bitch her due
that maven Cassie torn in her windy threnody

Ἀγαμέμνων
very steadfast with a little bit of soda his filament
a tear drop thinks tragicity a mere epitome of doubt
greekly sparking his antecedent is dense in upper land
hasn’t the matter some hand in the myth of echo or
later seemed to crust a valuable entity shipping out
and what quarrel with Thetis’s son stole Briseis and
plunked her in his tent fuming the rageful sod so big
and haughty spear demon caused even greater ruin
a whole era masked in his gold persona not deeming
others in his way driving his car forty horse down the
plank and Boom back to sea watching behind the Burn
while back home brewing something maleficent dark
wayward souls barking hoarsely in the reedy fens
can ancient books reverse his unforetold fortune nay
home rent night sick the fool in his trust cups his soul
strained by envy’s tridented ghoul and haply up stairs
to the bath climbs the churlish dog his end undivided
growling wrapped in crimson soaked sheets his corpse

(variation 1)
Oh bury me not on the lone prairie dumped it
were it not for the kids Orestes and Elektra vengeance
would not a written book be the players in their cothurns
and chitons like well draped linen haberdashers chittering
in an attic dialect about the main article while the splash
muffled in the bath receives little or no attention the epic

development writ in blood on now desiccated parchment
oh what the hell ivy girt verse in running trochaics
tongue lashed diphthongs and a rumor of envy amok
death's ruddy firmament with its massive cancer growths
like dendra issuing from the miasma and hybris of it all
the messengers themselves caked in offal and pus
riding bony nags across the brimstone paths
talking with their rudderless mouths about the Ruin
flashpoints of little consequence the bitter alimony
due to the still living in their silken rippling skins

(variation 2)
Mein junges Leben hat ein End schwerpunkt
all knives and smiles the cloaca gang comes at me
in dreams surfeit of obbligato and stress always
violence in the least word a fixation on the girls
took what I could when I could in the field and the
sea roaring echoless *las muchas muertes* colloidal
collateral conjunctive you name it the spawn of hell
furious and atrabilious of a generous dawn the rosy
fingered bitch scrofulous scorbutic ant heap
of the human mind labyrinthine uterine trench
delicacies to the contrary what did the playwright
know and how many acts and scenes to spill blood
and mop the floor and dust the mantel piece and
sell the books and who's making all those speeches
flowery ornate and greek especially greek why
the way they stumble over the deck chairs arms
raised high and appeal to a chorus of katydids
for the final runrun reversal of fortune AOI

(variation 3)
***Akagamunaš* from the fair uplands where heather**
blooms purple and hyacinth vies with narcissus
thither too am I known strongest of Mycenean
kings and golden mask and ornate curled beard
you know me by these marks and off to Troyland
I wended with my bro' cuckold Menelaus fought

there we did ten best years of our lives and cursed
the priest I did and claimed Achilles' girl as my prize
damn the lot of them *blffstxxx!* watching sea's angry
roiling waves bile-green eat the beach of its beauty
and Cassandra too earn for my keep mad thing that
she was standing atop the stairs doing the future rant
beware them Greeks and their foul smelling restaurants
well wouldn't she get it in the end her tongue still lolling
toppling down the stairway all threnody and hums
ain't nothing I can do to push back the black curtain
to keep out the hive of insects anxious to have at my eyes
to on my knees beseech Klytie to hold off her wrath
it's all miasma the dessert of the gods *blffstxxx!*

(variation 4)
whiplash grammar viaduct to the seven heavens of legend
lore strum strum strumming the ancient lyre for a verse
or two Oh tell me Muse-y all about him Master Bigger
king of Mycene the lion-gated how many his gilded masks
how far he'd go warring fiercely haughty arrogant bastard
sniffing in the offal for an image of his own ruination
out there among those damned by hybris head-down in mire
the polis on his back like an empty attic wind blown dusty
him just heaving his guts out in the tub mercilessly done in
by his floss-haired honey of so many years now a serpent
hissing directives in his deaf ear and celebrating a mass
piqued to hate by some uninformed eye in the wall
that he did this and that on such and such a time who knows
exactly where and the cliffs roared the secret to the skies
and some goddess always on the hunt to off some guy
took it to heart and had herself dreamed into the chamber
histing her hussy little skirts and Pow! so he gets it
all for a bit of catharsis that makes the audience feel "good"
and they pass around the worn play bill and act shocked grieved
miffed and it's winter outside and the snow has begun falling
really hard in mile high drifts burying the land of plenty

(variation 5)

hasn't many years to go before and language strung out
on its variable loom how to catch with any precision this
epic sense now all but lost in cloud works suchness and
viability singing high the notes and drumming palms out
beneath the heat of day heights of drowsy silver splendor
making love on the sandy spit embracing the unfathomable
waters of now longing has its distance and an algebra of azure
tilting deep into the delta functionless as chrome in light
to regard air where it is most narrow where the heavens
seem to barely weigh and suddenly the attack dazzling
crimson splashes over the canvas of pure abstraction why
is this falling why is the mouth filled with liquid salt so very
fuzzy in the scheme of irregular verbs and shame faced
the one who is most familiar is the stranger Herself she
who sparkles in the fission of destiny like no other resembling
the at once new attitude of the recent dead in their insignia
of marine astrology and isn't that even the extra inch one
had never surrendered unless to suspicions of nostalgia
when echo is the slightest reverberation in glass the tin-tin
of an all but forgotten childhood in the mountains of vertigo

Ἐρῖνύες

furious as debacle in mirror-spin they come rushing
through the tiny funnel at the bottom of Olympus
chthonic and infernal goddesses three wailing *shreee!*
one for the number it takes night to complete
two for the excess of time after eternity has ended
three for the hour after death which is forever
they dance the wild moonlight avenging human error
mostly words committed the wrong direction sounds
hissing sibilant in the unholy eve promises unkept
syzygy buzzing dreams rent in two and doubled over
sheets sopped with the draining sweat of madness
is it ever pure are there dewfalls of utter innocence
does grass at first understand then by mid morn fail
to comprehend the lesson of unerring light that storms
the eye crazing the demonic urge to overcome the good

ululating souls in despair hanging from invisible limbs
vowels of distracted impurity bleeding from the leaf
black is all they see black black black black black
and when the next day comes which is never and
if a new light signals on the anatolian hill
and if a new light ***shreee!***

(variation 1)
Alecto **the unnamable beware!**
smothered in kisses greets Sweetums at the door
shuts the windows that open on the periphery
turns on the gas and lights the match
and all the books in the house turn to cinders
and the puddle on the floor hisses and steams
and the stairs give way to the Stygian portal
what did I tell you?
it's all your fault you didn't listen

(variation 2)
Megaera **grudging you your existence**
stomps on the marble base of your lies
shatters your omniscience with a single flit!
groveling at the hem of her peplos you whine
begging for one more chance and her furious wings
whip up a cyclone around your senseless head
not even Athena with her kind grey eyes
can come to your ransom, Joe
you've forfeited everything
it's not a bible it's not a mayan inscription
it's not archeological evidence it's not the fourth dimension
it's not anything at all not even the long ride home
Sunday evenings when you didn't know where you were

(variation 3)
Tisiphone **vengeful destruction**
there is no aftermath no other worldly reckoning
only the destroyed cities of man
the ***cadillac*** **the** ***chevrolet*** **the** ***pontiac*** **and the** ***mercedes-benz***

still smoldering in their great metallic graveyard
gone the famous purple haze
gone the peace prize and the poet laureate
nothing but shibboleth and doggerel and maniacs
carrying portable nation states underarm
ready to blow up at the least suggestion
and the alphabet and the dewey decimal system
and the library of congress cataloging rules
all turned to nonsense in the enormous waste yard
where incinerators burn 24 hours a day
ridding the world of its pockmarked histories
in a fuming disregard for manners and science
blot out the names Κλυταιμνήστρα and Ἀγαμέμνων
erase the stock exchange and the diplomatic portfolio
let Ὀρέστης have his day!

"Ουκ ειμι Ὀρέστης!

XXI

THE TRANSFORMATIVE VISION

"…for the essence of the transformative vision
is that the sufferings of history themselves constitute
the process of transformation"
Josė Argüelles

under Indra's white parasol you worded
whatever it was you meant to say in dream speech
            countless times wrestling with your demons
cut glass unfaithful girlfriends bad acid trips
drunken driving above all
          suspended in your last year of college "pot bust"
or staggering home shoeless after a jazz night
   in the unconscious
            how could I make out your face screwed
oddly into the black wall of time evanescent

it was mine as well impossible to divine
the truth of the hour the numberless minutes
from the time we were born
until that afternoon on a San Francisco street corner
ave atque vale
the hollyhocks and painted stones
that lined the driveway   the folding chairs where we sat
waiting   the gravel and the plum tree in flower
and on the other side the weeping willow's mystery
who would be the first
dead from the start in our Mexican shirts
to proceed into that endless tunnel
sending back nothing not even an echo

illuminated windows where history occurred
the successive empires of sand and glass
tabulations in Linear B or mayan hieroglyph
where the one is greater than the ten
and all the grass in the world will not your finger hide
assumptions about the larger sky where cloud states
transform willy nilly all afternoon
come evening the tin can cries in the hidden alley way
voices smaller still huddle within the leaf
something sick between the covers a trembling lapse
envisions one dimension after another
proceeding to the nth infinity of post-modern time
let me hold you shaking ever so minutely
eyes turned inside out and nowhere to find the sun
that was the time of the long-bow and
the huntress keen Diana the goddess her aim
for sure was at you glorious stag in your summer
brimming to release number from the mortal count
and the afternoon was never long enough its song
like a gorgeous red thread leading out
through the empty palace on to the meadow
which the planets magnify with light by day
was the song we would always and ever remember
the pyramids the silver plane the jungle wet with rain

we both agreed that history has come to an end
man had exhausted his ability to perfect himself
beside the polished machines of τεχνη
lay in small muddy pools the rudiments of his soul
bits of sparkling mica and cheap rhinestones
this the poem we will write together both in this world
and from the other this the shattered epic
fragments of paean myth and hymn floral games lyric
a word here a phrase there the archaic deconstructed
whole echelons of unremembered verse
see! circling like great birds of memory
in the adumbrating heavens of Thoth the mercurial spirits
like troubadours who translate in all tongues
longings the immense trajectories of galactic yearning
to wake and perhaps never to wake again
beside the Other in some cryptic depth labyrinthine
the shadowy form of the enormous Unfulfilled
dizzy from such heights drowsy splendor imagining
ports of a meridian greatness teeming with gods
and warehouses with the merchandise of beauty
maps unfolding over lawns of chthonic mystery
showing us where to go in sleep and how
to revive the recollection of the Underworld journey
encounters with beings masked and unmasked
capable of narrating endlessly the epos of the soul
in its struggles to free itself from the mind's
purgatorial prison house however enticing
and there we were in the midst of shadows
playing for keeps with a grammar of narrowing air
flowers fields trees and rivers commanded
by hosts of bees and other winged sprites
to breathe! azure indigo and pure blue
suddenly you inherited a Toltec stone and became
your own idol and marched in processions
of brightly painted fans and quetzal feathers
vaticinations no one but you could understand!
let me hold you shaking ever so minutely
in the center of town bustling below the four-faced clock

we shone oracular and strange perceiving
in all directions an exciting destiny was approaching
women shining with lustrous waters
whose wild and white bodies were ready to embrace
holy mendicants prattling riddles about the end of time
or with warnings about the next invention
deities to ordinary beings invisible to us
like vast opened doors of language and thought
how could we sleep the eight hours of night
how could we sit in on lessons of geography
and history knowing them to be hallucinatory junkyards
were we not the mayan twins Hunahpu and Xbalanque
the vedic Ashvins or the Dioscuri Castor and Pollux
abiding in golden chariots symbolizing sunrise and sunset
trees hills birds everything even the underworld
was growing bigger and farther from us
and we were in a swirling reddening and wild
every minute was a myth a diagram to puzzle
and then to destroy repeatedly in our amaze
when would we go to the ant hill when would we
hunt and when would we be returned to the jungle
I remember waking one hot summer morning
the pool with its jasmine fragrance and the sky
scudding clouds calling us remotely
we walked unconscious from the ant heap
and went into the waters and for seven years swam
and tired of the waters we lay on the sands and dried
another seven years and adolescents big eyed and curious
we became either one or nothing in school with maps
compasses feathers great black boards
upon which were written the rules of all languages
you had a dizzy spell a nose bleed your eyes rolled back
let me hold you shaking ever so minutely
I cradled your head afraid of the oncoming darkness
if someone called us it was the avatar behind the door
what were we to do which was the book to learn
there was music fife and drum and viol a voice
singing in a swooning rush *we understood it*

in the next life the one that follows the residence
in the House of Darkness   in the life that follows
the long afternoons in the running grass
or in the life that suddenly commences in glass
            rippling through large shadows
in the sky formations that occur in the eye
    of the Nymph Echo   wherever there is talk
of what happened *before*   listen!
        in the veins of the cyclopean walls
voices multiple discordant
        that is the lesson of history
            there is an edge to sound and beyond that
how many times did we walk to the library
        chattering like howler monkeys
            running our fingers along the rim of time
watching the four seasons revolve in half a minute
before our very eyes   *white pink green yellow*
            and invisible cascades falling on marble
splashing liquid orients in the small air
                walk to the library
the lesson of history and memorized
            orationes of Cicero *gesta* of Caesar
and between the pages you entered the 4th dimension
    and wrote back after the millennium how you missed me
we took x-rays of our favorite city
        we would never be lost without it
if we fell asleep during the reading
            the teacher's mesmerizing sibilance
it was among the hedges in the back yard where we woke
still hearing her sybilline verses urging us
            and the rusty sound of a lawnmower
going over and over like a mantra in the ear
        winged insects and the distinct whisper of heat
what a summer that was and the stars!

"The corresponding development of Mercator's projection system (1541), in which terrestrial geography is plotted into squares, aided

in the transformation of nature from a wilderness into an intellectual field-pattern, and finally into real estate."
One Death and Seven Death defeated
Xibalba destroyed in the instant your nose stopped bleeding
in a flash everything happens synapses synergy wave lengths
the great wall the bottomless cistern and the jackals' dumping yard
it's graduation day 1956 pomp and circumstance and
Howling Wolf is singing *Smoke Stack Lightning* and the material
world is a thing of the past green reveries of a gone
looking at the Mississippi valley from the observation deck
of the Burlington Zephyr this was where La Salle and Father
Hennepin first heard the chattering jay and the Manitou
from his post in the topmost pines wrapping a robe of many snows
and five sheets to the wind and feeling immense
the train's insistent wheels clackety clackety clack
trees hills birds everything even the underworld
was growing bigger and farther from us
five ten fifteen years hence in the clip of a nail
enormous distances yawned open and the you and the me
who we had become talking journeys through colleges
aspirin wards insane crematoria the soul unsewn
writing book after book on the back of postage stamps
eating the remains of the small air
making the universe narrow a back room for ghosts
and still in our little sailor suits abracadabra on calle Tula
side street of watery Tenochtitlan counting dust immersions
vacant mansions of the desecrated Aztec moons
twenty and five years more hence exhausted
staring over the edge of a flower filled barge in Xochimilco
hesitancies a largo of sad European music
buffalo spirits tattooed to the vanishing cliffs
the long afternoon winding down
traces of the dead teenage Boddhisattva warrior
in the spiritually dead metal of Colorado
or it is even more remote as far back as 14 billion years
in Saint Mary's hospital on 2nd street SW
or it is orange blossom sunset color
pasted like sandalwood over the back yard

of 11870 Lucille Street   you know where
or it is the many volumes of Toynbee's Study of History
or it is nothing more than a footprint in the flowerbed
a conjecture of nightmare
where does everything go
ashes
a rain of ashes
an arpeggio

"He pretends to have designed and drawn everything on divine orders in his travels across the world."

XXII

JUGGERNAUT

"In Pukār, our town,
A whirling bee can't tell a woman's eyes
From a pair of blue flowers
Opening in the moon's reflection in the water"
Cilappatikāram

everything falls apart
what the mind is capable of
and what the mind utterly fails at understanding
are the same
crushed by the rolling wheels of time
maze of flowers fragrances bees aiming for the heart
secreto de amor compelled by hundreds of deities
onslaught of stellar whirlpools at midday
richly caparisoned elephants swaying on the royal road
horse drawn chariots without number under yellow canopies
somewhere in their midst king of the gods Indra
dead drunk lurching under the gemmed white parasol
on either side dimensions of *apsaras* seductive and sweating
blaring conch shells ankle bells clashing cymbals drumming tabla

for a hundred years this noon hour stretches in a riot
of cosmetics kohl henna lip gloss rouge lacquered nails
sandalwood paste smeared thick over bared melon breasts
tintinnation of the high pitched flute and OM chanting
by the thousand bards who line the monarchic thoroughfare
crowds dense with devotion and incense wafting black clouds
into the intense heated air that none can breathe
palm frond fans waved by copper skinned slave girls bought in Chennai
do nothing to quicken the stifling meridian atmosphere
nobody is anybody in this throng everybody is absent
the crush of human forms wild with witless ecstasy
moves as a tsunami wave across the city in its rectangular math
umbrellas made from the eyelids of *rakshasas* steam
beneath them courtesans and the hundreds of royal wives wilt
as flowers that can no longer hold their heads in a hot house
an odor of immense and lush decay pervades the festival
a labyrinth of colors saffron yellow mauve violet rose swells
like a mirage produced by the billowing tides of incandescence
blowing out of the doorways of the magnificent palaces
each in form and content like mountains of sugared candy
sultry eyes the pupils baked with desire peer through
the honey scented haze in search of the perfect lover Krishna
the ear fills with the deafening roar of an unseen orchestra
cinema love songs blare out of the cornices of hotels
it is an orient of spectacular and cosmic proportions
heaving buttresses and arches of polished stone into the sky
from which perch richly decked jewel crowned monkey gods
whose deft paws scatter red powders into the four quarters
of a heaven that seems to be painted like a massive paper
with threatening sulfur streaked thunder clouds rippling
just above the heads of drugged divine kings parading slowly
on their heavy draped mounts everything moving at lizard's pace
across a sun burnt paving stone in all directions dimensionless
no end to this infinite procession punctuated by the cries of peacocks
dancing in mid afternoon drizzle and the rich aroma of earth
lifting through groves of yellowish-white *champa* flowers into the ether
nobody has recall of the morning dew stained and flush pink
when the wheel was set into motion by mendicant Brahmans

reciting all four Vedas and the eighteen Puranas in mellifluous tones
when great dust balls arose from stables where the steeds finely
bedighted were readied for the concert of the altars
fuming with holy fires and banners smoking into the horizons
and the enormous pearly sea conch with its roseate ear
set forth the summons resounding as far as Mount Kailas
where dormant Uma still deep in a sultry perfumed sleep
barely stirred lifting a heavily serpent-braceleted arm
who was there to recount how the cars of the Sun glistened
moving out from night's ancient mansions into the empyrean
which is the shadowless house of the Unformed One
no one can recall how the day sped from its dark eternity
through the wakening among red lotus buds and the clamor
of distant oceans echoed in the nymph's earlets like salt murmur
cascading through the gilded fingers of the Merciful Goddess
and how mushrooming from invisible abodes the crowds
speaking the twenty eight Prakrits of the subcontinent
painted daubed bejeweled and scented with musk and sandal
no one distinguishable from the other dazed in a rain of yellow pollen
hypnotized by the world's myriad gaudy cinematic allures
among them girls scarcely adolescent hiding in themselves death
wrapped in costly silks and wearing their hair in towering pagoda shapes
on their hips blue lotus blossoms emit intoxicating fragrance
exulting in the enormous reference of smothering heat
who doesn't swoon at one time or other in the lush tropical syntax
from mid morning when the rush began and the array of ministers
of eunuchs dancers and mimes everyone as if a figure from a mural
on the walls of the Ajanta caves hardly aware of the person
or the passage of time embalmed as it were in great hives
honeycombs of intricate waxen chambers in which gamblers
some with dice others with dominos displayed on great carpets
cheat and swindle one another sweating in costly raiment
and the constant murmur of those paid to enchant and entice
filling the head with tales of colorful nonsense and pornographies
becoming drowsy with alcoholic drinks or sweet opium Bang
a dream a kinetic depiction a deception of being born and living
running before eyes half shut in illusory slumber the acts
of individual existence mummers dressed as humans performing

the various duties and businesses which involve the time of life
money passes hands in great sums women suddenly appear
marvelous and cunning barely clad bodices falling from the breast
rubies ensconced in deep navels nipples heightened to excitement
theft of mind enormous whisperings in endless corridors
being led through the inner sanctum of palaces the size of suburbs
where in the world is the outside where is the unfinished procession
smell of horse manure elephant dung rotting fish undone beds
stained yellow with sex play sashes drawn over wall-length windows
and the drone and hum of bees unraveling girdles and bow-strings
darkening hush passing from consciousness into trance state
flower petals falling inertly from withered victory garlands
memory now dim of daylight and the throbbing of drum and cymbal
specters of demons flying through the air in a dash to overtake
child brides living goddesses from the Himalayas and rape them
in cloud houses where anvils work to create menacing thunderstorms
no one is possessed of right thinking only error and human delusion
triumph of painted symbols of loud and roaring music of heat
and the broad way now quakes and cracks from the weight
elephants sway drunkenly out of line horses start on rear legs
bells ring dissonantly shrieks of women obsessed with obscenities
what is the cause of being why is the air so narrow and grief
swarms of poets and panegyrists who imitate and paraphrase
the polished epics of yore hem the deity in with their rant and babble
cacophonous ramblings and descriptions of the heretofore
what should remain ineffable and sublime defiled by wanton words
no one realizes the twilight of existence is upon them
cages of crickets swing back and forth inside covered wagons
parrots on the loose mock the two-legged entity with his own tongue
bright plumaged indigo moss-green ruby crested cockatoos
circle above the terrific din covered by rugs of powdery mire
to discern an identity in this miasma to pretend to individuality
on and on the procession continues into defiles shadowed by cliffs
which reach into the heavens and the astrologers with their charts
make predictions of celestial catastrophes that govern a man's fate
an inebriate laughter spreads contagiously through the throngs
and the girls in whom death dwells slide lasciviously flower bedecked
into the arms of the unsuspecting exchanging long wet kisses

**biting the supple throat releasing mephitic discharges deep and sweet
how great is the clangor at its acme which is at the same time its nadir
jesters and buffoons run lithely seeming to be everywhere at once
embracing the women-folk in the round dance the *ras-lila* of Vrindaban
for a moment everyone feels divine in the awesome presence
of something someone greater than themselves the Unformed One
ears ring with a chancery of harp and lute sounds eyes blissfully close
it seems the ocean is at their very feet prepared to drown them
in the rushing waters of Being for this is the day that never ends
this is the day that never ends
moonbeams
watery azure reflections
infinite lulling ripples
photograph of light
darkness the indwelling**
secreto de amor

the nature of the dream
**in the temple of the white elephant
in the temple of the unborn sun
who is wearing the mask who kneels
before the deity of the swarming bees
who speechless makes appeal to the burning air
to the ghats of purifying baths
that is I in a faint becoming pale and absent
losing memory of any language
being tossed a shadow wavering on a liquid surface
illusory image of a thought
the utter nothingness of childhood
in what life did I commit this error
in what transitory state did I *imagine*
and then to come to possess *this* consciousness
in whose house am I sleeping
do you enter the chamber of silences
drawing the curtains of whisperings
and beside me lie drawing from my breath
the red thread that leads to death
and mouth to mouth confess who you are**

the other the blank manifestation
the devotion to the Nameless
wet petals your locks
darken on your white brow
your fingers tighten the chords
of the stringed instrument the first
and third notes strike perfection
together we descend
inside and out the same *being*
there is a drizzle of pollen
a lone bird purple plumed cries out
eerie phantoms across the water
echo some indistinct words
fragrance of the yellowish-white *champa*
in the temple of the young white god
in the temple of the meridian deity
JAGANNATH

I dreamed we went to the great city Maturai
in the middle of the night its broad paved ways
teeming with coopers goldsmiths iron mongers
and mendicants who come from up country
seeking refuge in the sanctuary of the Tathagata
separated from each other we became *other*
ghouls inveigled us into distinct labyrinths
I was taken by the golden goddess who feeds
on the newly dead in the crematoria
and you gone forever

"I didn't know she was a goddess,
Had I known, I wouldn't have gone there."

XXIII

THE AMBIGUITIES

"Now may the dawns, the daughters of sky,
shining afar, make a path for man"
Rg Veda

is it from Tiresias we get this news
the who have drowned
the who have survived the passage
the recent dead the unaccounted for
writing this page as if it were the last day
how to go on from here deploring the Taliban
and the paragraph in small print where it says
our immortality be forever denied
what did we think when we arrived in Kabul
walking up and down something called Chicken Street
nothing but rundown shops and sheets of yellowish dust
had Alexander the Great been here before us?
planned to visit Bamian the place of shining light
with its great Buddha statue now blasted to bits
the itinerary was changed
sick on a houseboat in lofty Srinagar
at no time in our lives can we ever be sure of anything
the climb up the Himalayas to Leh Ladakh
in a bus held together by rubber bands
breath taking views and sublime Thikse Gompa
and what follows this life if not the unheard Sound
landed in Amritsar holy city of the Sikhs
felt like an oven air so thick a knife could cut it
the golden temple shimmering in its history
when everything becomes distance and dissolves
in a drizzle of yellow pollen
beware not to step on the slightest living thing
moving in and out of a hallucinatory traffic
of elephants and ox carts on the way to Agra
vomiting in the fetid bushes outside the Taj Mahal
Shah Jahan washing his sins away

a picture postcard of the remains of his love
and in the footnotes information about the soul
its whereabouts and a reckoning of its antecedents
but what is to come of it remains unknown
                had I written *sulfuric flames*
instead of *yellow pollen*
          would the poem be different
and if I declare *"I am not Orestes!"*
          would the Furies be placated
would there be innuendos undetected
would the past as we remember it be altered
and if I step perchance on an ant heap
to which hell and for how long would I be sent
rather it is four in the morning everywhere
dawn's prehistoric streaks daub the eastern sky
who wakes us is the turbaned bus driver
in whose eyes an eternity of shale persists
opaque as a pagoda inscribed in darkness
our destination in the world's highest mountains
where we will be suffering our karma
is just eight hairpin curves away

ambiguities that persist a lifetime
why wasn't the turn to the right taken
why didn't you choose the one with the red hair
instead of the brunette with freckles
why couldn't you make up your mind as to which
language to speak with clarity when summoned to court
because the rest of your life you'd be hankering
after the redhead the she-devil in command of breath
why couldn't you decide to play the large stringed instrument
why did you linger behind when the rest rushed
with enthusiasm to worship the deity of light
and yet you did settle for the poem about everything
because you could not decide what to leave out
Taliban deplorable Bamian blasted to Buddha obscure
statue bits four in the turbaned eastern driver sky dawn's
vomiting in shining Mahal fetid hairpin curves paragraph

suffering denied in Kabul immortality small print karma
rubber bands walking itinerary rundown sheets of yellowish
shops something Srinagar changed houseboat elephant
pollen sulfuric drizzle sick bushes Taj innuendos ant heap
shale lofty pagoda have drowned who have unaccounted
for survived where it says called a visit to anything sure
of a knife so thick dust before Alexander the lives distance
dissolves sublime views like an oven could cut shimmering
temple Great remains its history slightest thing ox Sikhs
living itinerary postcard forever arrived morning light

when the worshipful deity was nowhere to be found
and day's waning luster a fade orange pale on marble
twilit passageways into literatures as yet unframed
you were reading sleeping as you dreamed once more
the brother-dream threatened at his isolated desk
ambiguously positioned between metal and paper
what was the weight that gravitated darkly downwards
holding a grammar of silence and looked up and a voice
not recognizable speaking in parables prophetically
denouncing as ever the political delusion will it be
a catastrophe without warning a new system of numbers
flights of flame using only the eyes to direct syntax
between unfiltered spaces when suddenly in thick braids
the red-head who devours men's breath and heard
a hissing like steam coming out of the envelope held
in her white hand stands erect shadowless before you
ambivalent as to which twin to address which one to
unravel in a pool of inky liquid undefined words
of a thesaurus dissolved and wrapping a garland of
immense pearls becomes spuriously naked shivering
her great green Kali eyes hypnotic and profound
begins her serpent tirade using a language of red coral
undoing grain husks that litter the narrowing air
noon spent the syllables become more and more vague
unintelligible sput-sput-sputtering spitting glottal
stops saliva drenched consonant clusters enormous
diphthongs borrowed from vedic times begins to dance

hopping on one leg at first then with both shoving pubis
out inviting the swarms of flying insect deities with its
musky damp odor that fills the room and finally yes
gives the envelope still hissing steam to the brother
in question the one who invented his own book of genesis
who rising from his desk now arms dripping sweat
papers sticking to the skin involves the other self with
a gesture unique and sublime but ambiguous as to intent
is it the darkness of the unknown hemisphere or the fever
diagnosed as *"mother"* which is meant by this hyper correction
time slides into an ellipse orbiting his skull which is also
the other brother's the one talking dialect in rippling glass
a tombstone away from the childhood once shared

the apparently fragmentary nature of this composition
the apparently fragmentary nature of this composition

who have drowned, the
who have survived the passage, the
Tiresias a woman for seven years
has *seen* these things has suffered for it
and we are both here and not here sacking volumes
for a single reference to verify the light
that summons us through the windows of thought
writing this page as if it were the last day
who was a woman for seven long years
a prostitute who understood the language of birds
for striking a pair of mating serpents
the following summer in Morocco
the unmitigated unforgiving darkness
Tangier Rabat Meknes Casablanca
infestations of flies garbage piled knee deep curbside
sheer whiteness of the endless noon heat
sluggish ceiling fans named Dido
blind alleys of the medinas and above all
stench of the brightly splattered tanneries
do we have to live through all this again
forlorn beach at Casablanca and the dead aquarium

malformed children begging at the crossways
was that the summer Nixon resigned?
while the king lies in state in a gilded coffin
and above the seamless sky goes on forever
relentlessly azure terse somber
strong death wish afternoons like this
waking up to the haunting cry of the muezzin
invisible counterpart of the circling gull
concrete barrenness of the airports in the simoon
suffocating poison wind deep yellow dust and sand
to whom do we submit on our knees brows to the ground
just what *did* Tiresias say to Ulysses?
there are these conflicting versions
is Dante's the correct one and how will we know
like a super nova it all collapses in an instant
we were never there we were never here
kingdom abandoned by the gods malformed kids
peering through the slats of eternity
ambiguous planets cycling out of orbit
myths of Atlantis shipwrecks and madness
incomplete maps of the universe
compass of a fading imagination
ambiguities wherever one turns
indefinable colors
sleep
one never comes to terms with it

what follows and what is forgotten and the mind
turning on its own bent axis shifting through purgatories
of sand and red powders looking for the perfect image
to anchor itself to come to rest for a brief moment
when light and the lozenges of a soothing otherness
nothing to no avail keeps moving restless between
two opposing poles to act or to accept and let it be
shifting across topographies of exacerbating heat and
cold by turns mountainous or rolling fetid plains
a savanna or a jungle cries of unknown animals night
splendid beneath the sky of another planet not ours

how did we get here who summoned us what was the intent
to continue traveling sleepless nights in abandoned airdromes
looking for ticket stubs lost credit cards useless wilting
bouquets or bars at four in the morning lights blinking
rasping cigarette cough talking talking talking to some
Buddha be-alike with great advice about the next
life the one that's supposed to fulfill enlightenment
writing telephone numbers on the back of match books
looking forlornly out the window at airplanes taxiing
a light drizzle loneliness and the absolute emptiness
of a misunderstood moment which is all moments gathered
in the palm of a mendicant's hand at the doorway
wondering if this jacket too tight is really yours shoving
through anxious impatient queues to board still another
aircraft bound for the next existence on the Tunisian coast
where Dido burnt herself and trying to recall exactly
the lines in Virgil but at this hour and in this rush of
dirt and curses memory becomes a sieve a dribbling
mesh of half-words phrases out of context broken reeds
snatches of melody and lipstick and you cannot recall anything
with the sort of exactitude required for self defense when
you appear mysteriously hailed into a court beneath a
sluggish colonial ceiling fan and dreaming indeed yes this
is a circumstance you hadn't counted on and peering through
eyelids burnt by too much alcohol and cigarette smoke
pushed and shoved by others who like you are in the same
state of mind which is to say total confusion and ambiguity
the no this can't be your body and search all the pockets
graffiti of the brain tissue paper for a tongue gagging on what
is anything ever transmogrified is what we read in the papers
ever substantiated by the cuneiform original are we headed
straight for one of the bolge *of Dante's inferno not knowing*
for what sins and which is the pronoun to employ now addressing
your superiors or others in command and the clouds fill
the many empty windows and the aircraft lunges & lurches
through powerful wind currents and you think Jesus this is it
But it never is and in a sweat you transfer from this dream
sequence to the next not bothering to see who the passenger

sharing this ride with you is and what you personify and
why you are wearing this *mask is open to interpretation*
a quetzal bird calls out in the dark of night abject you lower
your head amidst a storm of parasols descending from seventh
heaven to the first levels of the mortal realm powdery mirage
through which cities of antiquity seem to stagger weighted
by the erroneous engines of history the sound of distance itself
crumbling like a ruined tower you can no longer ask yourself
why you are ambling in this rubble of the archaic and the nub
of eternity in the guise of a blasted tree trunk stands in your way
cannot decide which fork of the road to take undecided as ever
if only if only what   *a hotel room with a disheveled*
bed and a dirty lavabo   *streaks of mud*
trying to recall how you got in here without a key
where are your shoes?

a date with a call girl named Tiresias
talk of Apollo's shafts and the fear
dare you sleep in "her" arms?

how many are the recent dead
the consumptives
        those wholly devoured by cancer
bone and brain
terrifying excess of mortality
you walk gingerly lest you step on the slightest being
hence deserving the *naraka* of the Jains

in the back room of Webber & Judd's drug store
sharing a cherry coke and a grilled cheese sandwich
with the call girl of choice the lights dimmed
the windows smoked as by desire
both of you conscious of the ambiguity
of sex roles during intercourse
yet neither of you fully aware
that you have exchanged identities forever
listening to the small rain patter on the palm leaves
in far off Sri Lanka

the apparently fragmentary nature of this composition
the apparently fragmentary nature of this composition

XXIV

DE PROFUNDIS

Nemo sine crimine vivit

the end which is also the beginning
come full circle
"by the grace of Ahuramazda all that we did"
suborned by some nameless deity
to eat dirt or is it the music
that makes us larger than ourselves
what are the greater entities?
what are the depths?
what is the Fierce?
in all that we do a lyric madness impels
both absent and present the mind to a further remove

for hours counting , lotus petals dropping , one by one ,
into the fathomless pond , criminally insane deviant ,
perverse darkest bottom , maelstrom of the sea of being ,
howling , storm tossed , indigent , at a loss for words

this is not my domain these are not my Greeks!

fueled by litigious thoughts , rankled feelings , dis
possessed , constantly harassed by , againbite of inwit
, moving among the moveless , unformed beings ,
larvae , phantoms , succubi , the incessantly unborn ,

amphibian ancestors of human delusion , prowling ,
snake slips tied around the waist , the Oracle
pronouncing , syllables of unwonted darkness ,
incomprehensible , oonga-boonga , sulfuric wastes ,

in the underground , blasts of miasmic air , pollution ,
adore the goddess in the tiger skin tunic and red eye
she is the Veda beyond the Vedas! Redhead at AMOEBA!
morass of earthly confusion , bedeviled by stinging sprites

that whelm , the conscience with misbegotten deeds ,
shifting from bog to marsh , unillumined ,the native soul ,
haunted by the tom-tom , of the hourglass drum ,
that heralds , wanton thievery and highway robbery ,

cinnamon and ginger on the tongue , robes of heat ,
around the pounding temples , makes its weary way ,
from birth to rebirth in this , nether gloom , hash ,
shots fired in the unending , night , sacrificial flares,

maidens , tied to stags with enormous antlers , and
decorated with totem skins , and bridal pendants of teeth ,
that dangle to the belly , white , with soothing ointments
never certain what is, passing before the exhausted eye ,

to hail a car in this , confounded traffic and , pestilence ,
to remove the self , from the barrage of signals and , red
projectiles , hungry for some , unidentifiable meat a , sugar cake
, the synapses fail to deliver , messages of right thinking ,

laying the body down beside , the centuries' old banyan tree ,
from which hang , brooding , the , relics of a republic
make no music unless it is the circling of the Spheres!
insane , predestination , fogbound circuits , illusory hiatus

, the mind , desperate and impatient , is , a solitary confinement ,
inability to fathom such, depths, and to resurge , employing
whatever , means , broken chassis , arroyos where , tires
still spinning , chariot of the gods , upended , to rebirth , again

the wheel set into , motion , perpetual , turning , burning ,
ultra violet rays , gyres that require no language , a thunderstorm ,

what if it lasted , and the afternoon of a life , time , supposing
latest signs , a sky replete with beaches , devastated by desire ,

on the edge , where , everything is sprung , grasses , infancy ,
fingers lost , wooden wagons deserted , sidewalks of culver city ,
small red balls , painted toys in the eye , flight through horizons ,
of smoke , hills of , nostalgia , dead movie actors , riding saw horses ,

how did you get your hair , to look like that, in Pacific Palisades , a ,
swiftly impending sentence, using a pole , the boatman , pushed ,
through the sluggish , waters , listless cargo of recent , dead , all
colors cancelled , is there a special tone , do you spray it , red?

joined a cult , numerous and tiny gods , climbing on Uma's shoulders ,
RAGAZZA , strutting down the main , drag , moon on each hip ,
bag of unmentionables dangling , strong odor of sex , as if an island ,
cut off , drained of all impulses , left there inert , legs wide , apart ,

seeping darkish stain , evening in all its , sad glows , a dog's lonesome
whine , doors open and slam , shut , no one in sight , a firefly , solitary ,
hovers over planet , Venus , just above the house , Uma awake but ,
lifeless , trees , cows , verdant meadows , all in a medieval dialect ,

there! up up and away , inside the body , lunar ruins , like white ash ,
four to five tablespoons , let linger for a year , or so , never meant
to touch , HER , will be harsh , painting the backside with henna ,
mandalas , chakras up the spine , baby Krishna , kohl around his eyes ,

you will from this , point , on , the natural soul moving , between spheres ,
chanting , the way north americans do , we are left saddened , by
circumstances , hair stood on end , chilling , manual evisceration ,
in front of the public, library , lifelike Radha puppet , GOVINDA!

at the end of the special assembly everyone is dismissed sent home
to question nothing walk out of the car move over into the parapet
sit down at the outdoor café smoke a girl who is passing by just now
frequently do things not conscious of fondling the self in public wanting
the woman on the big wall-size poster facing the screen where animated

versions of Rama and Sita are running like crazy through an ovarian
jungle making hissing and sibilant sounds alternately as in the epic
translation by Valmiki whose name means ant-hill if you are up to a
cruise in my buick 88 he asks the girl he is smoking who is a pulp and
gracefully demurs the question to a later date maybe in the next hemisphere
when the moon pasted against a large white thigh evocative of high school
love letters sent without a return address but always haunting the song
as if from DE PROFUNDIS mentions that the girl was just thirteen and
visited by a holy ghost while at matins blanched her eyes turned back
into the cathedral of her brain and started speaking pidgin to the cassocked
brethren just back from dewfall how can that mean anything being evicted
from heaven the avatar using disjunctive vowels stuttering into his pipe
never would have guessed to inhabit this body in particular or to save
souls fiction really leaning against the smoke column and she engenders
a sort of hate between them and causally getting up and putting her cinders
out in his eyes calls him Romeo you creep crosses the street despite rush
hour traffic swiftly speeding heated metal animals all but grazing her
in the nick of time she arrives at the library to look up in the big pictionary
the meaning of the world "bolgia" puts it in her purse applying a heavy
swath of pizza flavored lipstick and nonchalant as any goddess in a sewer
makes her way through the wall drilling into the set of dreams labeled
"for eyes only" and meanwhile the guy is left behind in arrears stomping
out her butts in the corner drug store waiting for the cue that begins
literary discourse it's only a remedial joke between defrocked academicians
and frustrated linguists a puzzle to make poetry of the ruins of language
moving ever shifting through red spectra into the eerie galactic outback
where if nothing else longing and its fluted echoes drift infinitely until
SILENCIO!

kept walking until we got to November
stopped to rest on the old court house lawn
next to the rusted civil war cannon
to have a smoke passed around the Lucky Strikes
took a deep puff inhaling into the lungs
how brilliant that instant the sun shone
glinting off the various metal receptacles and glasses
no one could have guessed which of us was already dead
left the cellophane wrappers on the grass

rolled over on the back to take it all in
the enormity of space reduced to this inch
a crucible of fire between the fingers
trying to remember the poem from this morning
as the nicotine snaked its way through the brain
laughter from some other planet
maybe a block away below the neon sign
advertising women's hosiery and lingerie
the poem from this morning snaked its
between the lingerie and the prosthetic limb
poised against the shop window about
a planet away just down the street a brain
which of us was already dead you know
next to the rusted civil war wrappers a cannon
between the neon letters of the poem
this morning already a galaxy away the girls
tittering in their neon lingerie and hosiery
how brilliant the instant sun in an inch
between the fingers smoking to laughter
heard as if from a poem just blocks away
downtown where the course in literature begins
on the steps of the store where they advertise
neon lingerie for the girls tittering in wrappers
tossed carelessly on the autumn grass
where November walked as far as the old court
a house away from the street where hosiery
tittering the girls in their scotch plaid
and big brass safety pins read the poem about
trying to remember taking the nicotine into deep
the lungs burning smoke going out through the nostrils
thin blue curling columns evanescent
in the instant the sun on its back taking it all
in the guys chewing blades of grass a dream
You are the highest Letter the unheard Sound!
when the walk as far as November and loud
the civil war cannon makes its echo neon
against the blocks away a planet tittering
girls taking the nicotine deep into their lingerie

where literature begins advertising wrappers
tossed carelessly on the smoking steps
where laughter now so evanescent as a dim
instant the sun its big brass safety pin
next to the rusted court house the old lawn
remember trying the poem just hours before
chalk dust fingers writing names in the air
across the street from the house where the guy
the first one who got shot accidently died
though it seemed unreal Lucky Strikes passed
around the store where a prosthetic limb
in neon advertises the window deep into the lungs
which of us is already a poem trying
to remember was it in this life it happened

from the depths too many books so many cries
from the depths forever learning what cannot be taught
from the depths errant shadows yearning for form
from the depths red lotus blue lotus twining air
from the depths which is ending never having begun
from the depths too many books even more cries
from the depths anguish of never leaving the room
from the depths the steps that lead up to nowhere
from the depths the mystical union unpronounced
from the depths the the the the the the the AOI
from the depths the crystal boat on black waters
from the depths rivers of flowers running from the eyes
from the depths the hand of disaccord tied backwards
from the depths the word for *mother* applied to grass
from the depths the Fierce the glottal stop the anomie
from the depths waking within the rippling glass of echo
from the depths sounding the third and fifth notes of despair
from the depths not understanding what is meant by heaven
from the depths to walk with fire to the edge of time
from the depths leaning over the great Precipice of eternity
from the depths to remain ever dizzy from the first love
from the depths becoming and never being the mask
from the depths too many books and a thousand and one cries

from the depths sudden loss of memory and number
from the depths looking up and seeing nothing but red stars
from the depths making one's way through a soundless music
from the depths from the depths from the depths from the depths
smoking the first cigarette
tasting the first kiss
wet & dark

adore the goddess in the tiger skin tunic and red eye
she is the Veda beyond the Vedas! Redhead at AMOEBA!

XXV

DIES IRAE

"aut pereunt res exustae torrentibus auris"
Lucretius

as at first from the start and the betrayals
and jealousies and cannibalism and untruths
and the smoking house and poisoned libations
poured on the concrete surface of human error
fusion of distance and longing aching the beyond
wearing sandals of grief hardened to tears
why am I ever this soul rounding the cape
tattered and siren-deaf tied to the mast of unreason
sutures woven into the back of the hand a simplex
mankind in its inch of dung sweating the noon
when eaten by its own fiery ellipse the galaxy
returns with its instantaneous Paricutins
nothing to the touch a statue regrets its marble
decaying in a saffron light of endless afternoons
somewhere in the meat shop of Greek history
which is father reading his Sunday edition of Excelsior
comic strip fainting echelons of wormwood
under the bed the immense Unknown of alcohol
and the invidious solution to breathing step

**by wavering step like the drunken id of Zeus
shapes of illegitimate planets manifest brightly
at the top of the stairs like raw unlaced emotions
can abracadabra and silence balance so delicately
and the work of pushing the eye to its limit
seeing "seeing" the *terribilitas* of the human interior
carpets like maps of the cosmos spreading
through and during dolorous dust storms of time
*"or things perish burnt up by the torrid blasts"***

**mummified kings with upright scepters adolescents
steeped in camphor parrots' wings gold of four kinds
bales of strands of hair or silk soothsayers embalmed
in alcohol blocks of mountain size salt courtesans too
drugged to stand straight on the street corners hands
burning with eternally lit cigarettes philosopher's snared
in the lattice-nets of their concupiscent eyes like multiple
heavens the weight of mustard seed dwarfs bearing
statues of sand moveless in the rushing crowd of traders
dead from the heels up and who still prattle stock market
quotes as if they were poems of the ancients girls no more
than eight years old balanced on thin tin scales playing
all manner of instruments lutes harps flutes cymbals
one-stringed viols and holding the tune at the eighth note
so sweet and harmonious as to melt the skies coppersmiths
beating unconscious metal into shapes like vine-waisted
women supple as the south winds that bear cinnamon
to the cremation fields ashen bards propped up by fishing
poles reciting ageless stanzas in unison like a loud roar
of bees maddened by the perfume-drenched hair of love
slaves brought up from the cataracts of the beyond and
immense granite structures forty stories high with tiny
window holes that cast shadows over the great teeming
plazas where eagle-faced priests prepare for immolations
incense in thick bluish columns jutting like chimneys
into the infernal noon heat of the City of DIS**

so we wended southwards through lush unknown jungle

paths inclement nights swarming with flying insect hordes
the moon's wan light barely visible through the liana maze

at once a stone appeared four billion years old black basalt
around which an aura of whitish powders wafted
could this be the sign we were looking for the signal divine?

both Verna and Dickie set to quarreling over the purport
of certain eleatic verses harsh words turned to light blows
and soon on the ground both of them fought until naked

the monistic theory of one unchanging invisible thing
as the single property of the universe this we considered
lying on our backs smoking on the small wooded hummock

evening which always comes silently unawares wrapped itself
around our shivering corpses as strange orange globes
filtered through the racing galactic cloud works

one cigarette divided between the three of us to last a life
wonder what the gods who have been raised on violets
have next in mind for us trekking aimlessly through the stars

with only an antiquated grammar as a guide to the Underworld
etruscan milestones tamil epigraphy fallen to dust heaps
chthonic echoes as our heavy heads list into a dank sleep

instead of meeting Popeye on the beach we chance encountered
him in a sordid bar on the dangerous outskirts of the great city Maturai
nor did he in the least recognize us for he was deeply fallen in sin

sitting there side by side and laughing even though you are dead
we recounted our Friday nights when Mom would cook us hamburgers
and we'd listen to Brahms' 4th before going out and getting drunk

attributed to a metaphysical poet the arcane verses about the garland
of bees swarming the beloved's hair piece fragrances of jasmine and
campa flower the moon struck waters of her absolute reflection

grabbed the guy by the hair yanking him across the temple precinct
all the time someone plays a one-stringed instrument in the sand
then started kicking him mercilessly in the name of the goddess

side by side with the Greek and Italian poetries I consider the Tamil
their equal in refinement complexity and depth *then from Modesto*
take Maze Boulevard due west straight to the fords of Avernus

hard to believe that in this narrow space between the bottle-brush
and the dense overhanging of the fig tree is the entrance to the
infernal quarters where you can still see us sitting close together

nor were we so quick to divide the world laughing as we were
watching the guy being dragged to the statue of the goddess
pulling his hair out and sobbing all the way down Maze Boulevard

confusion and innuendo as always the minute you pass through the mirror
long corridors going backwards and emptiness of an unusual kind
as if the color red were stretched to its limit passing into space

and even farther southwards past the cloud scraping peak where
the temple to the monkey god still stands battered as it is and the port
where the Yavanas landed exchanging myths with blue-skinned Dravidians

standing at the end of the earth buffeted by fierce trade winds and tides
what could one do but expect the worst what with Joel and Fred fighting
in the dust what a turmoil and the surf rising angrier and angrier

DIES IRAE DIES ILLA peering through a small portal on the temple's
crumbling southside her peplos in rags her hair like a ruined beehive
the goddess Parvati you could tell was preparing for another fit of ire

Gaia herself shook underneath and clots of blood gathered mysteriously
in the air just as on those Friday nights when Joe and I blind drunk
would recite snatches of divinely inspired meter to the amaze of all

a limit to everything an edge to all space so they say thumbing through old copies of the Guide Bleu to the various sacred places to be encountered when hitchhiking through the vast and tangled extents of Arcadia

it isn't here and it isn't there either that you most expect to be taken not by the hair nor by the ankles but around the waist a moment of pleasure then BANG! the downward plunge in Uma's fierce embrace

the scene of the murder:
spread out on a broad plantain leaf for all to read
the whispered intaglios the cameos of hidden hair
excess vibrations in the yellow creeper as if a deity
lurking witnesses the flash of life what passes between
the ears the unplanned trip over the western hills
like a saffron robed mendicant stopping at decrepit
inns or wild groves to consult the Oracle the sudden
event of purple twilight and long hungry nights open
to the mass of traveling stars to wake perplexed what
happened why the blood stains and in the hollow of a
tree trunk a bag of rags do you ever ask why reason
doesn't apply you have to go into the dark alone

EPILOGUE

lesser than yesterday and the news
for why do we live in this wise on this wretched planet
cannot they see we are not as they thought
waiting listless on this border by the banks of this slough
each counting the fingers by which we number the days
and dwelling in such constant sorrow for the time that was
a greening spell for a few bright years of light
suchness of the novelty of breath and warmth
hauling our dream boats out of the murk
onto the grassy knolls to map and build a city
as it were the golden plat of imagination and accident
that was when
that was when if only we could recall with clarity what it was
when the tree grew crookedly out of the sidewalk
and thunder manifested in the midst of day
noons of a different splendor gathering in shade
to decide this that and the other
about who would get the greater share and who the lesser
and the arguing and cursing
wasn't that what happened in life
forgetting the origins forgetting the why of being here
never rightly understanding the because of fire
or the passing from branch to branch the illumination
mind that is the bright ornament of the species
literature has nothing to do with it
will this breath not also fail will not these words
uttered sleepwalking through the labyrinth
do they not lose their meaning and sound
as we embark on the passage across the dark water
or is it the way they set the knives on the table
or the nasturtiums and gardenias in wreathes
placed around the necks of the statues of deities
is it to place Śiva higher than Indra who clipped
the wings of the mountains

being oblivious of the hotel from whence they came
and diving into medias res created heroes who manned boats
and suffered the storms of fortune far from sweet sleep
and the goddess who hunted them down
how they sheared the shrubbery at eventide
reclining on vast lawns of ether to gaze at the star works
passing in celebration of nothing overhead
or being transformed by burning shafts into beasts
dimly lit by a human consciousness
so many worlds and divagations and ellipses
and books to read and pages to burn
sacrifice a black ram to the sun
place a small ivory bed in the temple of Hera

FIAT LUX!

Berkeley CA,
Mar 31, 2014 - June 1, 2014

REVIEWS OF FIAT LUX

One can read in *FIAT LUX* an epic poem as it might be dreamed; or perhaps
the dream of a culture in which the epic consciousness has been repressed, yet endlessly renews just beneath the skin of thought, in endless metamorphosis, pursuing mortal pleasure. Like a somnambulist, the poem plays out the passions and gestures of the gods amidst the tossed-off fixations of the day before yesterday, private joys and guilts steal sips of ambrosia from Olympus. In this world where Chronos is playful, Freud has shacked up in Pythia, one reads our culture's fevered dreams as oracles and symptoms. These prophetic anxieties are a babel of stories, of voices, of worlds, they are the fragments of languages, scattered like shattered beer bottles or amphorae along the highway. They unfold with a tragic tread in long incantatory lines, heroic episodes wherein sentences are dashed upon the rocks of punctuation, slain, sacrificed to Poseidon; or else, bristling with a *metis* both grammatical and psychological, continue on, journeying through strange worlds, Byzantium, Las Vegas, the pages of a book. "Let There Be Light": a demand, a blessing, a plea, a hope, or the condition for something yet to come.
- Olchar E. Lindsann

Fiat Lux is Ivan Argüelles' *Odyssey* through all human history and literature, as well as through the kaleidoscope of his own life memories. Often reveling in the wood nymph turned slut, he nevertheless manages, through confronting his own suffering, to sometimes approach deeper (higher) levels. For years now each new volume of his seemed the culmination of a brilliant life's work. Portions of *Fiat Lux* soar as high as any American poetry since Pound's Pisan Cantos. - Fred Bauman

There are beautiful mysteries in the genius that is the poet Ivan Argüelles—its sources, its aesthetics, its intents, its vision. As much as his twin brother, the renowned shaman/New Age healer, José Argüelles sought to save us with his vision, Ivan seeks to save us in poetry. *Fiat Lux* is the Harmonic Convergence of Poetry! To read it is to drop into all language, religions, myth, into our collective historical world knowledge and experience, into the Ocean. Once swimming, oh Heavens! For many Native American tribes twins are uncanny, *"the mayan twins Hunahpu and Xbalanque,"* and for our other cultures too, *"the vedic Ashvins or the Dioscuri Castor and Pollux."* Among other profundities, *Fiat Lux* is a paean to his brother, and to himself, left here. *"The soul unsewn."* Sometimes the poet is trying to open to José in the mother's womb they share, sometimes to him in death. And to their lives in between. This poem is of the process of transformation constituted by our sufferings through all history, as José taught, a memoir of the great longings and desires, of sex, a meditation on these, *"verbs drawn to love,"* which in the voice of a twin changes our perspectives on sex. *Fiat Lux* is most of all about language, the great gibberishes out of which creation and languages come, and the Law of Time: the universal factor of synchronization—another form of twinness. *"Both intellectual and uninhibited,"* as he says of the Surrealist poet Philip Lamantia. But behind Ivan Argüelles' vast knowledge and gift is the moving, recognizable sorrow for a twin brother dead. *"You gone forever."* - Sharon Doubiago

Ivan Argüelles is a poet whose oeuvre shines like a galaxy from the Earth. His words and lines are simultaneous with their own ascendancy. - Will Alexander

ADDITIONAL PUBLICATIONS:

ULTERIOR VISION(S)
Ivan Argüelles, 2011, Luna Bisonte Prods publication

The boundaries of time and form do not exist for Ivan Argüelles – they never have. While we've been occupied by the singular idea, trapped in a moment, Argüelles has refused to play by the rules or even accept the need for the game. His poetry exposes that idea as the provisional, phony construct that it is. Where most find chaos he discovers and sings sublime music. Earthy, psychedelic, profane, divinatory and sacred, these Ulterior Vision(s) are another distinct verse in a song that began nowhere and never ends. Through the day after day practice of such poetry this poet is living his work, an other life, an ulterior existence "in the electric dazzling we are." –Jake Berry
FIND IT HERE: http://www.lulu.com/product/paperback/ulterior-vision/18689254

A DAY IN THE SUN
Ivan Argüelles, 2012, Luna Bisonte Prods publication

The poems in A Day in the Sun say goodbye in a multitude of ways as the author's identical twin, the New Age philosopher/artist José Argüelles, simultaneously vanishes into the universe and manifests as absolutely everything. Great loss has always been a perpetrator of great poetry. Tennyson's In Memoriam sent that poet spinning into a questioning of all the tenets of Victorianism. Ivan Argüelles' vision—"small tokens memento / mori the whirring faces"—goes even further because it opens the mind to its ultimate ground in chaos. José Argüelles redefined the Western calendar and pointed the way to a universal harmony, a "convergence." In Ivan's work, the universe is expanding and contracting at once, and speech, far from clarifying, constantly returns us to the fact of Enigma. The world is wild, exciting, in constant motion, but also horrifying, painful, an endless blow to our Narcissism. Both visions can nourish and sustain, but A Day in the Sun beautifully offers us the elegiac, shadow side. –Jack Foley
FIND IT HERE: http://www.lulu.com/product/paperback/a-day-in-the-sun/18947483

CHAC PROSTIBULARIO
Ivan Argüelles & John M. Bennett, 2001, Pavement Saw Press (A book length collaborative poem)

Harold Norse states Arguelles is "the most outstanding poet since Pound for intellect," and when mixed with Bennett's pallet for sound, this collaboration written in five languages, fires up a new realm of concentrated stutterance for poetry. A Shakespearean punnery of language.

CHAC POSTIBULARIO ist ein ootwageous cuncocktioun ov linguadge in un estado ov tootal dis-schewelmento y abandonmento, un bytte loik der grayte Saynt John Lennon's immurtal "A Spaniard in the Works," et aussi un bytte loik le grand Saynt James Joyce's woiks, but a lot mo' apokaliptik ! Loines sech az "suerte de hermicranio, indeed, suckers bloom phaster in pfister hose" cunvince der reeder that die zwei Autoren ov dis ouvrage desurf to be hired to rekord saym, in its entoiredad, for der Nashunal Pubick Raydio, to be brodkasted in small porshuns every matins at foive dreissig ante meridiam. Durn on, dune in, dip in und oot -- in die wurds ov die auteurs, be "x-ed outta proporción bust- / ier with pasties flizzled to semble garters burning, jeezus arroz con 'poyo" ! Nut rekommendiert fuer reeders undah or ovah (fyll in der blank). –Anselm Hollo
FIND IT HERE: http://www.pavementsaw.org/books/chac.htm

www.ingramcontent.com/pod-product-compliance
Lightning Source LLC
Chambersburg PA
CBHW081132170426
43197CB00017B/2831
9781938521157